Being Boss

Being Boss

TAKE CONTROL OF YOUR WORK & LIVE LIFE ON YOUR OWN TERMS

Kathleen Shannon and Emily Thompson

Running Press

PHILADELPHIA

Running Press
Hachette Book Group
1290 Avenue of the Americas, New York, NY 10104
www.runningpress.com
@Running_Press

Printed in China

Published by Running Press, an imprint of Perseus Books, LLC, a subsidiary of Hachette Book Group, Inc. The Running Press name and logo is a trademark of the Hachette Book Group.

The Hachette Speakers Bureau provides a wide range of authors for speaking events. To find out more, go to www.hachettespeakersbureau.com or call (866) 376-6591.

The publisher is not responsible for websites (or their content) that are not owned by the publisher.

All photos taken by Sarah Becker Lillard

Library of Congress Control Number: 2017959126

ISBNs: 978-0-7624-9046-2 (paperback); 978-0-7624-9045-5 (ebook)

1010

10 9 8 7 6 5 4 3 2 1

**THIS BOOK IS DEDICATED TO THE BOSSES—
ANYONE WHO KNOWS WHAT THEY WANT,
OWNS WHO THEY ARE,
AND SHOWS UP TO DO THE WORK.**

(And to Fox and Lily . . . because you're the future.)

Table of Contents

Being boss isn't just a way of working— it's a way of life.

Hey, there. Emily and Kathleen here. Before we dive in we want to make a few things clear: we are successful working creatives who have bootstrapped our own businesses from the ground up (with zero debt!), but we're not writing a textbook on entrepreneurship. We're not going to tell you how to build a business model that works or guarantee a six-figure launch. And while we wholeheartedly believe that being boss begins with a confident mindset, this book isn't about manifesting your way to millions.

You crave the freedom to work the way you want, when you want, and where you want (and if you're anything like us, you want to work all over the world—from a coffee shop in New Orleans to the beach in Tulum). You want financial independence that will afford you the opportunity to make your own choices. And on the flip side of freedom, you also crave just a little bit of structure—a way to organize your day so you feel productive and efficient, but on *your* terms. And we know you've got some big ass goals; we want this book to be a guide in how to make those a reality.

Finally, the economy is changing. The landscape of how we work and who we work for is shifting. Self-employment is not just for the risk-taking bold and brave, anymore. More and more people are working for themselves out of necessity, practicality, or opportunity, but that doesn't necessarily mean they have it all figured out. No matter how you've come to entrepreneurship, you may find yourself needing some direction. You're just trying to figure it out as you go, and guess what—so is everyone else! This book is here to give you the guidance you crave and to let you know we're in it together.

Kathleen here! Growing up, I never imagined working for myself. The word "entrepreneur" was never a part of my vocabulary and I didn't come from a lineage of family business. In fact, my parents valued their day jobs working for the government, complete with fantastic benefits and retirement plans—a steady paycheck with a pension was the definition of "security." Growing up, I assumed the order of things was simple: you go to school, make good grades, go to an affordable in-state college, get a job with health insurance, contribute to a 401k, and save as much as you can. Once you have job security, you buy a modest car, get married, start a family, go on vacation once a year, work nine to five, come home, and watch your shows (our family's show of choice was the soap opera *All My Children*—we watched it on our VCR every day after everyone came home). Rinse and repeat.

I'm truly grateful for my pleasant suburban upbringing and what my parents provided for us, but I always felt a little bit like an outsider. My suspicions that I was different were confirmed when I was named "most nonconformist" every single year through middle and high school. While all my classmates were sporting Lucky Brand jeans and "No Fear" T-shirts, I was fearlessly rocking argyle socks, combat boots, and thrift store flannels. My style icons were Kurt Cobain and Gwen Stefani (and still are to this day, really).

I have always liked to think of myself as the rebellious youngest sister, but the truth is I've got a lot of Type A, rule-following, people-pleasing genetics at play. Sure, I let my freak flag fly a little when it came to personal style and creative expression, but I was still following the very safe path my parents had forged for me. I vied for gold stars from my teachers and hated getting anything less than an A on my report card (even an A- was anxiety-inducing). I graduated from college with a degree in fine arts and graphic design and got a job right away, working my way up to senior art director at a small advertising agency. Those gold stars turned into gold medals won at annual industry banquets, followed up by bonuses and high fives from my boss. In my twenties I had a mortgage and a 401k, and felt like I had made it. I was motivated to climb the ladder ahead of me . . . until one day I decided to build my own damn ladder.

MOUNT EVEREST MADE ME DO IT

I had been working as an art director for five years when I developed a bit of an obsession with Mount Everest. It started when I watched a reality-style TV show on the Discovery Channel about a group of adventurers attempting to summit the highest mountain in the world: Then I started reading books about Everest and watching serious documentaries about what it takes to climb the world's highest peak and the risks involved.

At the same time I had been keeping an online blog where I shared stuff like getting married, remodeling a historical home with my husband, learning how to cook good food, and all things adulting. Capturing, shaping, and sharing my life had become my hobby—and unknowingly, I was creating a personal brand for myself. Writing about the details of life helped elevate the mundane into something interesting, and—on the flip side—I was living more life so I'd have something to write about. I was surprised when someone besides my mom began to read my blog. I managed to attract an audience that not only liked reading about my life but would one day support my entrepreneurial endeavors.

Writing about my life intersected with my crush on the world's tallest mountain when I thought trekking to Mount Everest Basecamp would make a great story. And you have to understand, at that point in my life I had hardly been out of the country, much less to the other side of the world. Oh, and I didn't even own hiking boots. So along with all the things I needed to figure out to make this trek happen, I wasn't entirely clear on how I was going to take three and a half weeks off work when I got only two weeks of paid vacation time per year. But I started my plans to traipse through the foothills of the Himalayas by buying a plane ticket to Kathmandu, Nepal. I trusted that I would figure it out as I went.

I QUIT MY DAY JOB

I solved the problem of having limited amount of time off by quitting my job. It sounds easy enough when I say it here, and as of writing this book that was almost seven years ago. Hindsight has confirmed that it was a good decision, but at the time everyone was freaking out about who was going to pay for my health insurance. It's hard now to remember all the angst, but trust me—there was a lot of sobbing into a pillow and questioning my self-worth that went into handing in my notice. But I made that trek through the Himalayas, and documenting the experience on my blog solidified the newfound freedom I had found in working for myself—at first by becoming an invitation designer.

Years before, when I got married, I blogged about my tiny at-home wedding and the quirky Wes Anderson–inspired wedding invitations I designed for us. The invitations were shared by a big deal blogger (thanks, Joanna Goddard!), and she also shared the wedding itself on *Glamour* magazine's blog, which she was contributing to at the time. My invitations captured the attention of other offbeat brides who wanted invitations with a little more personality. I started designing custom wedding stationery and at the same time was submitting those designs to popular wedding sites, which introduced my designs to a larger market. I charged just $300 for the first custom invitations, but by the time I quit my day job I had more than doubled that fee and had hustled enough to replace my job salary within the first year of working for myself.

I had managed to carve out a name for myself—not only as a designer but, more surprisingly, as a branding resource for *other* people making a living being "creatives" too. Even though clients knew me for my design style, very quickly they saw that the way I directed a branding project was the same way I directed my own business—with a go-with-your-gut, unapologetic decision-making style grounded in a strategic mindset that had stuck with me from my ad agency days.

I was designing and doing business the only way I knew how, but I saw that it gave my clients a ton of confidence in return. They enjoyed our collaboration and how much I kept the big picture of their business in mind. It was as if they were getting the fierce big-vision wolf in pretty brand-design sheep's clothing.

After about a year of freelancing, I retired from invitation design and standalone design projects and opened a branding studio with my big sister, which we called Braid Creative. My sister had been the creative director at an advertising agency and thought she'd be there for life. When she became a little disenchanted with her own day job (even the most glamorous jobs have their downsides), I saw my opportunity to convince her to join me and double down on our strategic and creative talents. Together we built our own branding agency and team.

People ask us about the name, Braid, and we describe it as weaving together all the threads of their business vision. Whether they're a solo creative entrepreneur or a layered business, we're integrating their personality, voice, style, and expertise into every decision we help them make. On any given day our team is consulting, coaching, visioning, writing, and designing for our dream clients and helping them go after their dream clients in return—with a clarity that helps them really share who they are and sell what they do.

Along with documenting that life-changing hike through the Himalayas, I continued to share the story of becoming my own boss on my blog. I was writing about everything from how I was feeling, which from one day to another ranged from "I got this!" confidence to "What am I doing?!" freak-outs, to the more technical aspects of working for myself, such as how I managed my time and tricky clients. In the process I had positioned myself not only as the kind of person who has the freedom and courage to go on grand hikes that end with watching the sun rise behind Mount Everest but also as an expert in being my own boss. Plus, I attracted a tribe of other creative friends who were also working for themselves and figuring it out as they went. Friends like Emily.

70 percent of American workers dislike their job.

WORK HAS THE OVERALL LARGEST EFFECT ON OUR MOOD.

FEWER THAN ONE IN THREE AMERICANS ARE "VERY HAPPY."*

*www.nydailynews.com/news/national/70-u-s-workers-hate-job-poll-article-1.1381297
www.mentalhealthy.co.uk/news/1391-fascinating-happiness-statistics.html
www.theharrispoll.com/health-and-life/American-Happiness-at-All-Time-Low.html

Emily here. I spent my childhood watching my parents and grandparents do back-breaking work that they didn't love doing so that they could put food on the table. If you were to ask them if they liked their jobs, they'd probably say "yes" out of duty, but I could tell the difference. I watched them hurt physically, emotionally, and spiritually as I grew up, and it taught me some important lessons. My parents and grandparents modeled a killer work ethic; they worked hard to provide for their family. However, I learned a subtle message about how doing work you don't love can put a damper on your whole life. Doing work you believe in and enjoy is the difference between being happy and being ever-disgruntled.

As I grew up, this "Do the work" ethic modeled by my parents and grandparents manifested itself in my own life. In high school I worked hard to make really great grades, took advanced classes, and even took college courses. I entered college with my freshman year almost complete, like the rebellious little overachiever that I was. In college I routinely worked two jobs even as a full-time student, not necessarily because I needed to but because I liked to do new things and wanted to stay busy in the working world. I had no problem bouncing from job to job, as long as it held my interest and my boss was a good person; I loved learning about how retail chains operated, how small businesses made it work, and how they all got their customers to buy what they were selling. I was in college because I "had" to be; I was working because I liked being in business.

MY FIRST BUSINESS

In my first year of college I was presented with the opportunity to buy a tanning salon. You heard me: a tanning salon. Long story short, at the age of eighteen I became the owner-operator of that tanning salon (I can still smell it sometimes), making me feel like a total boss, even though I had very little idea as to what I was getting myself into.

I was in college full-time and running my tanning salon in Mobile, Alabama, in 2005. Less than a year after buying the salon, cleaning it up, and putting forth my first-ever marketing campaigns to make it awesome, Hurricane Katrina hit the Gulf Coast and my entire world (along with the world of everyone around me) shifted. My salon sustained minimal physical damage: we lost our sign and had some water damage. The hit came in the way that matters most to a small business—economically. Our clientele had bigger fish to fry than themselves, needing to fix roofs or assist family, and some even cut their losses entirely and moved away. For months, disposable income for the entire community was cut. I was just a kid and the pressure to sustain a commodity business in that place and time was a lot to handle, so I made the decision to sell the salon almost two years after I became the owner. But I knew I'd dove into something that would thrill me forever. Being my own boss and running my own business was in me now, and it would never go away.

That tanning salon taught me a lot. It taught me that being a business owner comes with lots of paperwork. It taught me how to be responsible for things like commercial property, contracts, and customer education. I learned about managing employees and a brand. Had I found my passion in running a tanning business? No. But I experienced something at an unusually young age that has fueled me ever since: what it felt like to be my own boss and to build something bigger than myself. I had found a passion in business. But somehow, these ideas didn't shape the rest of my formal education at all.

EDUCATION FOR A JOB

I ended college with a degree in geography, a certificate in geographic information systems (GIS), and a minor in art history. I loved geography because I have a deep connection to the Earth and the things that inhabit it. I envisioned myself becoming a professor who taught kids about the world we live in, or working for the National Park Service to conserve and protect land and wildlife. What grand dreams! But they were the kinds of dreams that weren't being fulfilled much anymore; the job market was changing. I mean, aside from a higher education, *a job* is one of the main reasons why you go to school, right? And for me, that's why the GIS certificate was there: that's where I was going to get a job, except I had no desire to be what a well-meaning professor called a "GIS weenie," which basically meant that I would spend years in a cubicle turning paper maps into digital maps, either for a private company or maybe the government! Ew. Educating children or frolicking in wild forests wasn't in my cards. I graduated more than a little heartbroken. Looking back on it, it's strange that getting a business degree never really crossed my mind.

MY SECOND AND THIRD BUSINESSES

Even though I finished school with a clear path in front of me, I had no desire to continue down it. I didn't want to be a GIS weenie. I wanted to be my own boss, and I wanted to spend my life doing something creative. I wanted to do something that I would really enjoy.

While wrapping up my last year or so of school, I started my second business. I had discovered Etsy and adopted it as the platform where I would launch and grow my first online business. In addition to loving business, I have also always been a maker. All of my friends had friendship bracelets I made. I crochet and cook and sew. Etsy gave me the opportunity to turn a jewelry-making passion into a money-making endeavor.

Etsy also provided a community that showed me how to be a business of one, selling what I make online. *Making for a living*, no matter where I was located. What a cool way to work! This job I had created for myself gave me flexibility beyond my wildest dreams, and I had a very fruitful couple of years growing my jewelry business online and in my local community. But as college graduation neared and the reality of life began to set in, I needed more than just some extra income, and I wasn't positive that my jewelry business was one that I wanted to scale large enough to fit our needs. My partner, David, was heading into his master's program, which offered a very small stipend, and it was up to me to pay the bills. Over the last months of my jewelry business, I had moved my online shop off Etsy and onto its own website. In high school I had picked up some website-making skills, so I did all the work myself: designing, coding, creating, and loading up content. *I had a blast doing it*. Before I knew it, I was spending more time tinkering with my website than I was making jewelry, and I had Etsy friends asking me to make websites for them, too. Two weeks after graduating I posted some website design services on Etsy and sold my first project. Thus, my third business was born.

It's important to note that by this time we also had a family, having brought a baby into our lives as well. Our daughter was almost two when I started my web design business; I wanted to stay home with her. I had already proven that running a business was something I could do and that doing it online would afford me the flexibility and freedom that I desired. But I was also responsible for financially supporting our family while David finished his education, so I had no choice other than to make this work.

In this third business of mine, I found a calling in helping creative folks start businesses online. I spoke their language and I knew what they wanted. *I was one of them*, and I spent the next six years creating websites for stationers, yogis, photographers, and other creatives who wanted to make their mark in the online world. But I wasn't only launching websites, I was helping them start and grow businesses that let them do what *they* loved, work from wherever they wanted, and live by their own rules. I built a sustainable, profitable business that did some good for the people I worked with, made good money that supported my family, and filled me with purpose that left me energized at the end of the day. It was also a business model I could scale and grow, satisfying my need to stretch and strengthen my business muscles. I increased my revenue, expanded my team, and never had to go be a GIS weenie (even though that unused education has proven to be essential in ways that I never expected). The sacrifices I made were different from the ones that my parents and grandparents made. I gave up organized benefits for flexibility. I gave up a dependable paycheck and low-risk employment for doing work that compensated me in ways other than cash. None of it was easy, but I can promise it's been worth it.

BECOMING BUSINESS BESTIES
Everyone always asks how our paths crossed.

Kathleen here. Emily and I became online friends in a time when you still had to clarify whether you knew someone from the Internet or "in real life." We read each other's blogs and left encouraging comments or inquisitive questions. Emily suggested that we video chat over Skype, and one time turned into monthly sessions. We exchanged information on systems and processes that were working and how to handle difficult clients, and we even got honest about our income and how we price our offerings. Our paths crossed in real life at a blogging conference and we began hiring each other as we grew our businesses—Emily hired my company to help her with personal branding and I hired Emily to help me scale my one-on-one services into an online course. We were also sharing clients and, in general, appreciated each other's work ethic and drive.

In 2011, we had an idea. We wanted to launch a weekend workshop in which we would teach creative entrepreneurs everything we knew about our combined expertise in branding, building an online business, and marketing it to attract the dreamiest of customers. And it totally failed. We got one signup and decided to call it quits before we sank any more effort into something that wasn't working.

Failed project aside, we still got together over video chat regularly to talk shop. We found ourselves talking about things nobody else seemed to be discussing out loud—from how much money we were making to how we juggle work and family. We openly shared business secrets and insights with each other. We became really good friends whose favorite topic of conversation was nerding out about business.

BEING BOSS: **THE PODCAST**

In December 2014, Emily proposed the idea of starting a podcast together. We were already creating content on our blogs, sharing what we'd learned with our following, and having candid conversations with each other and our peers about the work and life of being a creative entrepreneur. Why not hit record and release these conversations for everyone to hear? Emily has always had her finger on the pulse of business trends, and as grandiose as it seemed when she said, "Podcasts are the future and ours is going to change the world," I believed her.

Doing the work is what makes you look like an overnight success ten years later.

We started *Being Boss* as a place to bring our vulnerable conversations about work and life, our experiences as small business owners, and our expertise in branding and online business to others who were going at creative entrepreneurship, too. Together we'd chatted with thousands of clients and creative peers about the mindset, habits and routines, boundaries, and balance that go into being a working creative—and we were ready to bring those real conversations to an audience. We thought we'd reach a few listeners looking for guidance on how to go out on their own and make a living doing what they love. We were surprised by how quickly the podcast gained traction.

Within weeks of launching our first episode we hit the top of the charts on iTunes, quickly attracted a loyal following, and landed some lucrative sponsorships from like-minded brands who believed in our vision and our voice. We snagged interviews with accomplished entrepreneurs and our own personal heroes, including Brené Brown, David Heinemeier Hansson, Ramit Sethi, Chalene Johnson, and Melissa Hartwig, to talk about topics ranging from money and living a rich life to staying healthy as an entrepreneur, as well as personal stories of success and failure. We created space for our audience not only to listen but also to join the conversation and create connections—from online forums to in-real-life vacations and retreats.

To the world we looked like an overnight success, but we knew it was just the beginning of a new vision that countless hours of hard work had brought us to.

AND NOW WE'RE WRITING A BOOK. FOR YOU.

So here we are. Writing a book—something we dreamed about for years as part of our plans for world domination (mwahaha!) and a natural next step to what we're already talking about on our podcast. We're here to share our own experience, advice, stories, tactics, and to-dos that will help you make money doing what you love while being who you are 100 percent of the time in work and life.

Now, enough about us . . . *who are you?* Well, if we had to guess, we'd say you desire the freedom to work the way you want—on your own terms and your own schedule. But with that, you might struggle with creating structure for yourself. You're brave and you set big goals for yourself, but sometimes you're overwhelmed by all your ideas and what it will take to reach your dreams. You want to grab life by the horns, but sometimes you feel less than confident and too trapped in your head to get your ideas to fruition.

We know you because we are you. And we've worked with hundreds of creatives just like you.

Whether you are still working a day job with a creative hustle on the side, you are fresh on your path to working for yourself, or you have a few years under your belt—you can *be boss.* This book is for creatives and aspiring entrepreneurs (designers, photographers, artists, musicians, coaches, nutritionists, trainers, stylists, event planners, consultants, chefs, yogis, wellness professionals, athletes, performers, community organizers, etc.) who need more tools, advice, and inspiration to level up, hunker down, and do the work.

This book is going to help you dig deep, dream big, and take action. We're not going to show you how to run or market a business (though we are pretty bomb at that). We're not going to show you how to "get rich quick" by meditating and manifesting your way to success (though we are a little woo like that). The nitty gritty details of how to grow a team or launch a new product is another book for another time. Instead, we're going to show you how to set up the foundation to be boss so that you have what it takes to expand your capacity for success (as you define it!), cope with inevitable failures ('cause if you're behaving like a boss, you're gonna fail), and take responsibility for creating the life you want to live.

We suggest you read this book from cover to cover. We've included some of our best stories and tactics along with quotes, excerpts, and Q&As from our favorite creative peers and industry experts. You'll also find some worksheets in here—you can fill those out in the book— or you can download them at www.beingboss.club/book/ worksheets, print them off, and fill them out that way. If you feel challenged or stuck along the way—that's okay! Keep reading. You can always come back to it, and we hope you do. We want this book to become one you'll keep on your shelf, that over the years you'll reference, highlight, tab, and wear down with love.

And if you want more of us, you can follow us on Instagram at @beingbossclub or subscribe to our podcast on iTunes.

WE SHARED OUR ENTREPRENEURIAL JOURNEY WITH YOU. TAKE A MINUTE TO REFLECT ON YOUR OWN JOURNEY TO BECOMING YOUR OWN BOSS (EVEN IF YOUR ENTREPRENEURIAL JOURNEY IS STILL IN PROGRESS).

CHAPTER 1

What It Means To Be Boss

Being boss is owning who you are, knowing what you want, and actually making it happen.

Here's the deal: we don't believe everyone has what it takes to be boss. Not everyone is brave enough to actively create the life they want to live. Not everyone is self-motivated enough to take consistent, actionable steps to reach their concrete goals. But if you're still here, we think you might. If reading that little bit of tough love has you questioning whether or not you have what it takes, don't worry. We got you. The fact that you picked up this book, alone, means you've got it in you. And by the time you finish this book, you should be connecting new dots, owning who you are, and imagining a future in which you call the shots. Because *that's* what is at the heart of what it means to be boss.

The most boss creative entrepreneurs we know have a couple of key things in common. They're confident. They know what they want, and they know how to make it happen. They work in a way that's smarter, not harder. They focus on impact and strategy. They have no problem seeing the big picture, or breaking it down into a plan to get it done. They work like artists, makers, and shakers, but they think like entrepreneurs. They are open-minded and see their work as an experiment. Their work is personal, but they don't take failures personally. They value getting it done over per-fectionism, and prefer community over competition. They blend who they are—their personalities—into the work they do. They feel good about the money they make doing the work they love. They reliably deliver, and they hustle like a boss.

Here's what being boss is not

If we're going to identify the qualities of what it means to be boss, then we'd be remiss not to identify decidedly *unboss* characteristics as well. Now, if you identify with some of these it's okay—we do too every once in a while. But being boss is actively working against these low-vibing qualities:

- LETTING FEAR DICTATE YOUR DECISIONS
- BEING OVERLY NEGATIVE ALL THE FREAKING TIME
- BLAMING OTHERS FOR YOUR MISTAKES OR FAILURES
- PLAYING THE VICTIM
- GIVING UP UNDER PRESSURE
- SETTING VAGUE GOALS
- BEING APOLOGETIC AND FULL OF SELF-DOUBT
- LOOKING FOR EXTERNAL VALIDATION
- CARING WHAT EVERYONE ELSE THINKS

LIVING WHAT YOU LOVE

Being boss is about knowing what you want and being unapologetic about it. It's being who you are, nurturing your talents, and sharing them with the world. Being boss means doing the work to get you to where you want to be, even when it's hard or when no one understands. A boss owns it all, stands up for what she believes in, is brave enough to take risks, has the courage to make mistakes along the way, and makes big, beautiful things happen, even when the process doesn't always feel easy or fun.

Because life happens in that hot mess of a process. It's big and beautiful there, too. But only when it's something you believe in, when it's something that you find joy in—day in and day out.

Being boss is living what you love, every day and in every way that you can. You have to build a life you love as if it's your job. Because it is.

EVERY DAY I'M HUSTLIN'

Recently in the circle of creative peers, the world "hustle" got a bad rap and a little bit of backlash. Perhaps it brings up images of working late into the night and on the weekends and having no time for fun. Or it might even conjure up ideas of a mob boss doing less-than-ethical work to get what he wants in unscrupulous ways. That's not what we're talking about when we talk about hustle. We're talking about doing smart work to reach your goals, building a business that allows you to express yourself, making money doing what you love, making a positive impact on the world, and taking care of yourself while you're at it. Hustle is also about injecting those same practices, boundaries, habits, and gumption you put into your work into your life.

There are times when being your own boss feels so damn good—you're digging what you're creating, you're in the flow, and you know you're getting somewhere with your work. And there are other times when your big dreams and relentless ambition are just too exhausting. When you feel this way (because you will), it's time to put your big dreams on the shelf (right next to the airtight jar full of your worst fears) and just do the work.

Here's what our hustle looks like on any given day:

- WRITING A BLOG POST OR NEWSLETTER
- RECORDING A PODCAST
- WRITING AND DESIGNING A NEW OPT-IN/CONTENT UPGRADE FOR OUR NEWSLETTER
- DESIGNING A KEYNOTE PRESENTATION FOR AN UPCOMING TALK
- REFRESHING OUR BRAND IDENTITY
- WRITING AN OUTLINE FOR A BOOK
- SCHEDULING SOCIAL MEDIA POSTS
- EMAILING A PODCAST SPONSOR ABOUT OUR PARTNERSHIP NEXT QUARTER
- OUTLINING AND DELEGATING A TASK LIST (COMPLETE WITH DUE DATES) IN OUR PROJECT MANAGEMENT SOFTWARE
- BOOKKEEPING AND ADMINISTRATIVE TASKS

Listen, nothing kills the paralyzing power of self-doubt and insecurities like the act of creating something. We're not talking about launching the thing, or promoting the thing, or even selling the thing. It's in the MAKING of the thing, which can take the most work of all, which is why we believe in the hustle.

We want to tell you what our hustle looks like, but let us begin by telling you what hustle doesn't look like: finding purpose, planning, dreaming, wishing, thinking, journaling, reading, learning, researching, meeting, engaging, or Instagramming. Do these things matter for the success of our businesses? ABSOLUTELY. We spend a good chunk of our time planning, dreaming, thinking, learning, and meeting—because they're absolutely necessary to create the business of your dreams, but those things are not hustle. Hustling is doing the work that it takes to convert your ideas into something that takes shape in this world. It's all the things you're doing to rock your career or the avenue that you're taking to make money to support yourself.

You need both the vision *and* the hustle. You need a big picture *and* a step-by-step plan. You need work *and* you need rest. You need structure *and* you need flexibility. You need community *and* you need competition. Your capacity to live in the tension of the "*and*"—and your ability to recognize when to push and when to pull—is what will make you a creative, productive, and happier boss. And that's what this book is really here to help you do: find confidence and self-reliance in the blend and the balance of being boss.

With all of that said, we try to *not* glorify the hustle, but getting shit done is how you build a life you love. Sometimes that looks like spending a week working out marketing plans, rocking a client project, or building your new product line. And other times getting it done is more of a life hustle that looks like finally booking that massage, taking that vacation, or actually showing up at yoga class. The secret to finding some balance between life and work is to pair your work hustle with life hustle.

Life hustle is all the things you're working hard for, and sadly it's the part of the puzzle that most people push aside because work leaves them too tired and a Netflix binge is just easier. When you're done with work for the day, your work is not yet done—if you're hustling out your life, you will continue to nurture your relationships, throw down on that passion project (not for profit but for fun), and go on epic adventures. Of all the things that you do, create, launch, and make, your life hustle will always be the hardest but also the most rewarding.

It's not about making the hustle cool. Instead it's about taking action—establishing a habit that continually drives you toward health, wealth, and happiness for yourself, your family, and the people you serve.

THE FOUNDATION OF BEING BOSS

Shortly after beginning the *Being Boss* podcast, we began seeing patterns and themes in our conversations with each other and other creative experts. We started talking about these themes *all the time* and realized that they form the foundation of being boss in work and life. Each subsequent chapter of this book expands on one of these themes. It's important to note that none of them stands alone—they all work together and often overlap.

MINDSET: You can't be boss if you aren't in the right frame of mind. The challenges we tackle when it comes to creating a fulfilling career and life require the right mindset: having confidence in who you are and the decisions you make, seeking out motivation and inspiration, committing to big ass goals, trusting yourself to do the work, knowing and practicing your values, remaining positive, and tackling fear and imposter syndrome.

BOUNDARIES: Boundaries are the physical, mental, and emotional "rules" that you define for yourself. These rules keep you from feeling overwhelmed and overworked. Boundaries will also help you decide which opportunities you say "yes" to, what you say "no" to, what you let in, and what you let go. Boundaries enable you to carve out time to do what you want, prioritize what matters, and determine your own rules for working and living.

HABITS AND ROUTINES: If mindset and boundaries get you emotionally and intellectually prepared for doing the work, your habits and routines govern *how* you get the work done. From setting goals and establishing a morning routine that sets you up for success to taking care of yourself outside work, habits and routines are how you behave like a boss.

YOUR WOLF PACK: It takes a village to build a boss life and work, and cultivating a pack of just the right people is easier now than ever before. Your wolf pack will support you, encourage you, and assist you and will include your friends, family, mentors, peers, and collaborators. We'll share our insights into how to meet new people, nourish relationships that are mutually beneficial, and collaborate, partner, and ultimately work with others to build something really boss. Relationships are everything, and they'll help you go far.

YOUR WORK: As a creative, you work to make money doing what you love while staying true to who you are 100 percent of the time. This work takes dedication to your craft, unwavering focus on your goals, and reliance on your own skills to take you from dreaming and scheming about what's next to actually doing the work.

YOUR LIFE: As much as we love our work, we don't define ourselves just by the work we do or the bottom line in our bank accounts. The most admirable bosses we know prioritize connection, relationship, family, friendship, travel, and really good food (yeah, we like our food) over making money or being a slave to their Rolodex (if you don't know what a Rolodex is, just Google it). Bosses are curious about life outside work and use their resources to enthusiastically pursue what they find interesting.

BEING BOSS AT WORK

The word "boss" might make you think of someone who is in charge of a team of employees, but when we talk about being boss, we're talking about an attitude of owning who you are and being intentional about actively creating the work and life you want to be living, and the impact you want to have on the world. So you might be a one-person shop, a freelancer, or a small business owner with a team of employees; you might even have a day job you love (with a boss of your own), or a creative side-hustle you're aspiring to take full-time one day. No matter what your circumstances are, when you use the principles we outline in this book, you will be boss.

Being boss isn't necessarily about wanting to make a million dollars. It's about gaining expertise in your craft, truly becoming a master of your work, and then being compensated for the work you're best at. And hey, we're not opposed to getting compensated millions doing what we love, but when we asked our podcast listeners how much money they wanted to make in their creative career, they told us they wanted to make just enough to pay the bills and have the freedom to call their own shots. When we asked them to get specific about what that number was, we were surprised to learn it wasn't anywhere close to a million! In fact, for a big chunk of our listeners the yearly salary they needed to pay the bills landed somewhere between $35,000 and $60,000 per year (before taxes!). But whether you make minimum wage or five figures a month, we don't want you to make just enough to pay the bills: we want the work you love to support the dreamiest lifestyle you desire—whether that's a house on the beach, the flexibility to home-school your kids between deadlines, a job that leaves you plenty of time for hobbies, or simply being able to buy an off-season avocado for $3 without thinking twice about it . . .

Money is part of a rich life, but it's a small part of a rich life.

—RAMIT SETHI, *BEING BOSS*, EPISODE 57

In our experience, running creative online businesses has afforded us the flexibility, freedom, and cash money we desire to live the work and life of our dreams. We've successfully imagined our ideal days into reality by working smart, consistently creating content, positioning ourselves as experts, delivering quality work, adopting productive habits and routines, and employing systems and processes that keep our ships running tightly. We routinely look at what's going well and what's not, and test and change how we're working accordingly.

With creative work, it's your duty to do work that you believe in. Work that brings you joy. Work that allows you to express yourself in the best way(s) you can. You need to create, make, coach, guide, and share. You need to believe. You need to spread your soul's message far and wide through whatever medium you have at your disposal. If you don't, you're wasting your talents. You're not fulfilling your destiny. You're putting a stopper on your potential for happiness. By embodying your creativity, you're taking the first step toward living what you love.

As an entrepreneur, you have the drive to make money doing just about anything. You have a business-owning bone somewhere in your body that's pushing you to monetize, to make a viable business model. As an entrepreneur, you see more risk in not taking the leap than in taking the leap. There's magic in that.

You have the capacity and the ability to support yourself and your family. You have tools at your disposal to make it work—to reach an audience, share your passion, make a difference. If you can survive the challenges, the testing and changing, the trial and error, and the learning curve—if you have a real entrepreneurial streak in you—you'll make it. You'll make profit that provides for your life while doing work that you believe in.

You'll sacrifice—we all do. But the payoffs will be worth it. So what's at stake? Your happiness. The happiness (and health?!) of your loved ones, of your children. Your potential. Your here and now, as well as your future. We don't mean to be melodramatic, but everything is at stake.

BEING BOSS IN LIFE

Being boss is not just about hustling from 9 to 5 and then kicking up your feet with a beer and a bag of something sweet or crunchy (or both!) and that being the end of it. Instead, we believe that being boss in your work should be the catalyst for you to live the life of your dreams, and the life of your dreams is probably more complex and exciting than beer and snacks. Being boss involves a certain kind of self-defined balance between your career and your life that allows you to thrive. We believe in the "work hard, play hard" philosophy, and it's a duality that all of our favorite bosses share.

In this age of *boss*, gone are the days of looking up to the sixty-five-year-old CEO retiring with a gazillion bucks in the bank but no admirable

Being boss is different for everyone

Beyond the basic framework and overarching themes we've outlined for being boss, it's the details that shape what it really means to be boss, and those details differ from one person to another. This is a fact that we honor. We're giving you the framework that we use to set the foundation of being boss, but it's up to you to fill in your own details. We hope that by sharing different perspectives, including our own experiences and journeys and advice from experts in their fields, you will find the freedom to define being boss in a way that is meaningful to you.

Being boss is being accountable to my own values and vision above anything else. It means I wake up in the morning with a plan no one else is going to hold me accountable to, but that I choose to execute like my life is on the line. Because it is.

—CAROLINE DONAHUE, WRITING COACH AND PODCAST HOST, LOS ANGELES

Being boss is always about doing the work. To be boss is to follow through with your dreams, goals, and plans—instead of just fantasizing about the job you wish you had. It's creativity and commitment, inspiration and energy. Because when you blend both, you can build a life and business you love (and that loves you back).

—JESSICA WILLINGHAM, WRITER, CHEYENNE, WYOMING

Being boss is getting off the couch, putting on your running shoes, and chasing down a future where you call your own shots. It's saying yes to a future version of yourself that thrills and terrifies. It's showing up on days when the work feels good. It's showing up on days when it doesn't. It's being okay when you can't show up at all. Because being the boss is all about the big life goals we accomplish, but also what every day feels like along the way.

—JENNI HEFFERNAN BROWN, WRITER AND BRAND STRATEGIST, SAN FRANCISCO

Being boss means the absolute privilege of doing the work that I love, instead of grinding away at anything less than soul-stirring. It means defining my role instead of having it dictated to me. It means allowing myself the flexibility to grow and evolve, and having my business reflect that. It means learning EVERYTHING about starting and running a business, being brave, being curious, building a team, and doing what needs to be done every damn day—and loving every crazy minute of it!

—MICHELLE LEWIS, AUTHOR AND HOLISTIC HEALTH AND WELLNESS COACH, LAKEWOOD, CALIFORNIA

Being boss is all about holding yourself accountable and taking action in your lives. Doesn't matter if you're an entrepreneur, work in corporate America, or [are] a stay-at-home parent—being boss is a way of living your life that puts you in the driver's seat as opposed to riding shotgun.

—DOMINIQUE ANDERS, CATV PRODUCER AND BUSINESS AND LIFESTYLE COACH FOR CREATIVES, LOS ANGELES

Being boss is having a business that is in integrity and based on my values and beliefs. It's knowing that I have the power to change my own life, and helping others to empower themselves to do the same. Being boss is showing up just as I am, vulnerably, honestly, and powerfully.

—SHANNON WHALEY, BUSINESS AND MARKETING COACH, CAYMAN ISLANDS

Being boss is getting out of my own head and allowing myself to take control of my future. It is weaving together the things I love to create a sustainable business that supports not only my family, but also my wildest globetrotting dreams.

—LINDSAY FARRER, JEWELRY DESIGNER, NASHVILLE, TENNESSEE

personal qualities, family, or friends to speak of. Our kind of boss focuses instead on being a whole, curious, responsible human outside the realm of work, too, and such a life has more purpose than bringing home a paycheck.

Bosses craft a fulfilling life, which includes investing in quality relationships with family and friends—connecting and nurturing relationships with people who encourage and help bring out the best in them. Bosses insist on a healthy lifestyle in which personal health is a priority, including getting enough sleep, eating well, and listening to their bodies. Bosses have hobbies outside work that keep them learning and challenging themselves in ways that make them lifelong learners. Being boss means that you're intentionally multifaceted, and you have the capacity to have it all if you work hard enough to build a life that you love.

DO THE WORK TO GET WHAT YOU WANT

You're going to hear us say "Do the work" over and over again, so get used to it. Our motto and the thing we say every time we sign off our podcast is "Do the work; be boss." The two go hand in hand: doing the work comes first, and being boss is a product of that work.

Doing the work is everything that happens between the wanting and the having. It's the little steps that take you from point A to point B. It's not grand flourishes of awesome; it's the daily grind that moves you forward. In fact, the work is the most un-Instagrammable part of the boss process. Doing the work looks like getting out of bed, brushing your teeth, and putting your game face on. It's opening the file, making that phone call, and practicing your craft. Doing the work is living your life and doing your job. Consistently, persistently, every single day.

Here's the deal: there are a lot of books, programs, and blueprints that are going to make empty promises and set unrealistic expectations—we do not make any guarantees. We will teach you what we've learned from living as creative entrepreneurs, working with hundreds of creatives, and interviewing some of the most brilliant minds of our times, but it won't make any difference if you don't do the work. We'll shine a light on the path, but we can't walk it for you.

Does this give you deer-in-the-headlights anxiety? The thing that will temper the overwhelming pressure is twofold: a *commitment* to enjoying the process and *trust* that it will get you where you want to go. When you commit to enjoying the process, you're doing work that energizes you and living a life that you love. That may require a shift in your career, your role within your business, or your living situation, or it simply may require a shift in how you think about what you do. That's for you to decide—do the work. When you trust the process, you release worry and anxiety and find fulfillment. You release expectations of the outcome. The more you trust yourself, the more you turn into a self-reliant, awesome boss, learning your lessons and making strides every step of the way.

Doing the work is what separates the dreamers and the talkers from the doers. It's what separates the hobbyists from the professionals. It's what separates the amateurs from the bosses.

Want chicken alfredo made from scratch for dinner? Do the work.

Want to be a gold-medalist gymnast? Do the work.

Want to support your family with your creative career? Do the work.

Hit a snag along the way? (Because you will!) Get back to work.

If you're not willing to do the work, then put this book down now. We're done. And while you're off doing whatever it is you think is cooler than making your dreams come true, consider getting your shit together. We'll be right here waiting for you when you boss the fuq up.

For those of you ready to dive in, here's a promise and a warning: we promise that the payoff will be good. Doing the work *will lead you somewhere*. If you have a clear trajectory in mind and *do the work*, you will make it somewhere you want to go.

But we warn you that it may look like nothing you ever imagined. It will usually look similar, but rarely exactly like you planned. It may not be on your timeline. There are infinite variables pushing and pulling your efforts in directions that our small brains are incapable of comprehending, and that mystery is part of the fun. Being boss is a careful dance between getting clear and doing the work, and letting go of expectations and trusting the process. Get ready to hand yourself over to the lifelong game of being boss.

Ready to do the work? Let's get started.

If you're happy with the process, then the outcome doesn't matter as much.

—PAUL JARVIS, "PODCAST LIKE A BOSS,"
BEING BOSS, EPISODE 75

Being boss is owning who you are, knowing what you want, and actually making it happen.

- ARE YOU OWNING IT?
- DO YOU KNOW WHAT YOU WANT?
- ARE YOU COMMITTED TO MAKING IT HAPPEN?

CHAPTER 2

BOSS MINdSET

Being boss is believing that you've got this.

Carrie and Beth are hardworking women with day jobs, but both dream of becoming full-time photographers. Both experience the same issues as they begin pursuing their creative paths: they wonder if their dreams are silly, especially since they have perfectly good careers that pay the bills (even if they're not the most fulfilling); they're afraid of wasting their time on an endeavor that may not amount to anything; and they're unsure how to even get started.

Carrie decides to confront and navigate through her insecurities. She tests the waters and her own skill and resolve, investing more and more of herself into becoming the best photographer she can be and building a business with her expertise. She seeks out mentors and a community, and commits to learning and practicing. Carrie begins proving to herself that she has the ability to figure it out along the way. She falls in love with this endeavor (and, in turn, herself for being such a boss), and one day makes it to a place where she can leave her day job to realize her dream of being a full-time photographer, but much to her surprise she doesn't find herself in wedding photography, as she thought. She finds herself being a sought-after editorial photographer, getting opportunities she never dreamed of. The experience is exhilarating, fulfilling, and gratifying and totally freaking terrifying at times. She is tested in ways she never expected, but no matter the obstacle—whether inner gremlins or outer foes—she overcomes it, growing more and more confident in herself as she proves she can do hard things. She makes her dream come true and is a better person for it.

Beth, however, lets the questions and insecurities keep her from even beginning her journey. Comfort, even though it may not be as fulfilling, is less scary than taking a leap. *What if I make the wrong decisions? What if it gets too hard? What if I can't do it? I don't have all the answers.* These questions and truths are too much, so she stays in her day job until she retires, doing work she doesn't *love*, living and working by someone else's rules, and never testing her own capacity for success. Whether she accepts her fate or always resents not making the leap is no matter—the truth is that she lets fear and insecurity keep her from trying something new that could have been the most fulfilling endeavor of her life. She never chases her dream.

Beth stays loyal to her day job and career, but is not loyal to her own dreams of becoming a photographer. Carrie, by contrast, embodies our boss mindset: she doesn't let fear stop her from trying something new, she allows curiosity to fuel her creative adventure, and she doesn't let any inner or outer critics keep her from pursuing her dreams.

Your dream is your calling. You can choose to answer it or not. Either way, you have to own the outcome. Which outcome do you choose to live with for the rest of your life?

Now just to be clear, we're never going to tell you to quit your day job or that doing so will get you everything you ever wanted, but we will also never tell you to put your dreams on hold for the sake of what feels secure. Nothing is certain; when someone else is in charge of your paycheck, you can get fired. The company you work for can take a financial hit and your job can get cut. All without seeing it coming. Job security is most often just an illusion, so don't stake your happiness on it. Stay if it's fulfilling, not because it feels secure.

Around here, the criteria for a boss mindset is simple: you face your fears, you believe in yourself, and you make decisions. If you do these three things, *and do the work*, then you are unstoppable. You can set the path that you would be most proud to travel, and make an impact on the world around you.

If you *don't* believe in yourself, make decisions, and face your fears, you're not going to be doing the work you were put here to do. You'll stay where you are, with what you have, which is all good and fine if you've found your success, but we're guessing you're here because you know there's something more out there for you. We're going to start with helping you cultivate the *something more* that's on the inside. The outside will follow.

But we do need to take it one step deeper, because doing all the cool things in all the world still isn't boss if you're a Crabby Patty or Negative Nancy who's just waiting for the world to serve you up what's "owed" to you on a silver platter or are tearing others down to build yourself up. In addition to being a confident decision-maker, a boss also believes there's enough room (and work) for everyone, that a rising tide lifts all boats, and that doing good is better than making a buck or proving your point, which is where our definition of "boss" begins to steer clear of the mobsters and managers who give "boss" a bad rap. Our kind of boss chooses positivity over negativity (that's at the core of not letting fear and feeling like an imposter rule your decisions) and lives and works in a way that encourages others to do the same.

In this chapter, we're diving into a few dark places every creative explores, and serving up the boss mindset alternatives that will help you reshape your point of view to serve your best interests, which are success, fulfillment, and happiness. We'll explore facing your inner critic (which we call "fraudy feelings") and the fear of failure, which are negative mindsets that we all face. The trick is to not let them rule your attitude or behaviors. We'll counter those unproductive mindsets with their archnemeses: confidence and courage. We'll wrap up with some insights into how these mindset shifts will serve your greater purpose, along with some practices that we use to help us be boss, because it doesn't always come naturally.

WHAT DO YOU VALUE?

The core of the boss mindset is your *values* and your *intentions*. Your values are the guiding principles that direct you through life, helping you prioritize what's important to you and stay true to who you are. Your intentions are the purpose that you give to your actions, helping you infuse every move you make with meaning. When your values and intentions are aligned, your work and life will feel efficient, effective, and meaningful. Sounds pretty nice, right? Let's dig in.

VALUES ARE THE GUIDING PRINCIPLES THAT DIRECT YOU THROUGH LIFE

Values are the personal truths and principles you hold most near and dear—they're the things you would be willing to go to battle for. What you value often motivates the "why" behind the decisions you make and the actions you take. For example, if you value *courage,* then you might regularly do things that scare you. If you value *authenticity,* then you might have no patience for small talk or regularly question how things have always been done. If you value *security,* then you might like having a route mapped out and an itinerary in place before setting out on a trip. The best part of identifying, understanding, and practicing your values is becoming more at home with who you are. When you are unclear on what matters the most to you, you might find yourself feeling apologetic, scattered, and vulnerable to other people defining who you are and what you like or don't like.

Defining your values

There's a lot of chatter out there about finding your purpose and chasing your passion—and trying to find the meaning of life while you're there, *amiright*? Spoiler alert: there is no universal truth that gives all of our lives the same meaning. Joseph Campbell says it best:

Life has no meaning. Each of us has meaning and we bring it to life. It is a waste to be asking the question when you are the answer.

—JOSEPH CAMPBELL

Drop the mic, right? Bringing meaning to your life's purpose is a tall order.

Tammy Faulds is an amazing life coach who always lends solid perspective when it comes to defining, prioritizing, and living your values—and doing so gets us closer to answering the question, "What is the meaning of *my life*?"

BEING BOSS: First off, how do you define values?

TAMMY FAULDS: I use *values* and *strengths* to help clients get unstuck. The example I use is that strengths are in your DNA; these are what you're naturally good at (and are often talents we take for granted). Values are based on choice and help to "steer your ship" through life. For example, my strength of *empathy* allows me to connect with people on a deep personal level, but my value of *balance* ensures and reminds me to pull away after a coaching session so that I don't bring their story home with me.

BB: Why is it important for a creative to prioritize values (over, let's say, making a buck) when it comes to making decisions in work and life?

TF: To put it simply, your values are the GPS of your life. In decision-making moments you can lean on your values to help guide your behavior and choices. For example, when I'm triggered or pissed off and can't put my finger on why, I will pull up my core values list—which I keep on my phone—and evaluate the situation or person that's causing tension against my list of core values. This allows me to take a breath, pull out of the situation, and quickly hone in on what is out of alignment. Then I can decide on my best course of action. These check-ins work for these smaller (sometimes daily!) occurrences as well as bigger picture situations, such as leaving a job or a relationship. And note that when life is going well and humming along, it's likely because you're living in accordance with your values. Think of your core values as a constant in your life, which is a nice thing to have in this ever-changing world!

Being imperfectly human, we're going to stray from our values from time to time. When you need to make a decision like paying the bills versus practicing your values, ask yourself what potential challenges you face if you don't align with your values in this situation. If *security* is a value, then that might outweigh the headaches that come from working with a particularly difficult client. If *authenticity* is a value, then perhaps it's not worth it and you can lean on your value of *trust* in that something even better will come along by saying no to this one. But if you do decide that paying the bills is more important, then you can use your other values to set some healthy boundaries in the contract.

BB: What if a value feels more aspirational and not entirely true to who I am? How should I handle that?

TF: Be true to YOU. Aspirations are just that . . . aspirational. They're not necessarily true to who you are or to what has shaped your life. If you're struggling, ask yourself WHY you aspire to that value? Is it because it's how you want to be perceived by others? Or maybe it's how you perceive someone else to be and you want to be more like them. Or perhaps society at large tends to value it, so you think you should too. I've had clients say that they wish they could be more patient, but imagine a world filled with ONLY patient people . . . nothing would get done! So if you're more of a fiery person, honor that, embrace it, and use it to your advantage, because it's who you are and it's what lights you up!

BB: On the flip side, what if I value something (like money, fame, or power) that embarrasses me or makes me feel guilty?

TF: I find people sometimes slip into labeling values as "good" or "bad." I had a client struggle with *recognition*. She thought "doing good work" should be all the recognition anyone would need. But when she's not feeling recognized at work, then she feels bad about herself and wonders why she bothers putting the effort in. However, after getting in tune with this core value of hers, she was able to communicate to her boss that she really values recognition and would appreciate the feedback from him. And guess what—she got it and felt great!

I really struggled with *rest* being a core value of mine. I thought it sounded selfish, childish, indulgent, embarrassing—*and* it made me feel guilty. But the more I thought about it, I realized it's really who I am. I come from a family of nappers and I've always felt amazing after a "half hour of power." But as a busy event planner, I wore the "I worked 30 hours straight at that event!" as a badge of honor, proof of dedication, perseverance, and a "winning" attitude. It took me getting sick, *really* sick, for me to honor this core value of *rest* and make some healthier choices. The changes were small at first—asking for help—then morphed into bigger changes like when I left the industry completely. Not surprisingly, the pre-cancerous cells that my doctor was monitoring "magically" disappeared after I prioritized *rest* in my life.

Just like emotions aren't "good" or "bad," I personally don't think values are good or bad. The meaning we give to them and the stories we tell ourselves about what we value are where the judgment comes in. At *Being Boss,* you've

referenced how people feel about money [for example, "Money Mindset," episode 94 of the *Being Boss* podcast] in the same way—many people hate it, or feel bad for wanting more of it, and so on, but it's all in how you frame it. We can see money as evil or as freedom. It's all about perspective and what it means to YOU.

BB: How do your values help you make better decisions?

TF: Learning about my values allows me to make decisions with greater conviction. One of the bigger (and scarier) decisions I made was to leave a job I mostly enjoyed, but I couldn't figure out why I was feeling stuck. When I looked at my values compared to the company's values, the alignment simply wasn't there. This clarity allowed me to see that in order to find the fulfillment I was seeking, I would need to leave, and so I did. It wasn't easy, but knowing this truth made the decision easier. That's the brilliance of being in touch with this GPS of yours—you can tap into it whenever you need, and move through life with greater ease and confidence in all your work and life decisions.

BB: How do you integrate future visioning and your values when it comes to long-term planning?

TF: On the road of life, you—you gorgeous human being—are the car, your strengths are the engine, your values are the steering wheel, and your vision is your destination. You wouldn't plan an epic trip without knowing where you're headed, right?

To expand on my previous example, this was precisely how I made the leap from a comfy corporate job to something I *never* thought I'd do—entrepreneurship. I knew my values and I knew that in order to feel whole and complete I needed to align myself with those values in my life *and* in my work. That sounded great, but I was still floundering. What kind of job aligned all those values and strengths? I had no idea, until I started to analyze the common themes and came across "coaching," along with "leadership" and "teaching." I didn't know coaching existed in 2008 (it was still a buzzword at that point), but I was definitely intrigued. The more I researched becoming a life coach the more I realized this was my vision: an independent lifestyle conducted solely from a laptop that helped people live more fulfilling lives by having deeply transformative conversations. BOOM! *Connection.* That vision, born from researching my values and strengths, lit me up like nothing else. Once the vision was clear, all I needed to do was map out the path to get there. And honestly, that vision of me working from a beach house is what keeps me going in my darkest hours.

Vision pulls. Values steer. Strengths fuel.

—TAMMY FAULDS

Find your own values

1. Find a quiet space, clear your head with some deep breathing, and connect your mind and body. *Most important: do not rush the process. Start by making a sacred time and space to do the exercise—say, thirty to sixty minutes.*

2. Look at the list of values and circle the words that jump off the page and feel good to you.

3. Take a short break to connect with your breath again. Close your eyes and think about a time in your life when you felt fantastic, in the flow, and like everything was right in the world. Feel all the sensations and breathe those sensations into every cell of your body. Then open your eyes and go back through the circled list with that vision in mind. Which of those values were prominent in that scenario? Place a star next to those.

4. From the starred list, grab a highlighter and see if there are any values that are similar in scope and try to pair them off. Perhaps you have *truth* and *honesty* on the list . . . what do those words mean to you personally? How does the dictionary define them? Can you think of situations in which *truth* or *honesty* have played a role? Pit them against each other and see which one resonates more deeply with you.

5. Keep whittling your list down until you get to five to ten values. I ended up sorting my list into five "hard" values and a few supportive "soft" values. For example, *rest* is a hard value and supporting that are *balance* and *health*, because if I'm rested, then I feel balanced and healthy, and if I am not rested, well, consider yourself warned.

6. A final filter I like to throw on it is, "If money weren't a concern, would these values still resonate?" Or you might ask yourself, "Would I put up a fight or go to war to defend this value?"

7. Shelve it and walk away from it, but keep those values in your mind as you move through the week. See if they show up in your daily interactions. At the end of the week, revisit your list of values again and see if they still resonate. Once you feel you've solidified your list of core values, write them down in your phone, on a Post-it note, or somewhere else where you'll see them. *Know that you can always tweak them later if need be.*

Tammy Faulds is a holistic life coach based in Toronto, Canada. A certified professional coach, 500-hour Registered Yoga Teacher, The Daring Way™ facilitator, and meditation teacher, Tammy coaches people who have found success in their lives but are seeking deeper fulfillment and connection.

FIND YOUR VALUES

Abundance
Accessibility
Accountability
Accuracy
Adventure
Affluence
Agility
Alertness
Alignment
Altruism
Ambition
Art
Artistry
Authenticity
Authority
Awareness
Balance
Beauty
Belonging
Bliss
Boldness
Bravery
Calmness
Candor
Capability
Carefulness
Celebration
Certainty
Change
Charm
Choice
Clarity
Cleanliness
Cleverness
Closeness
Collaboration
Comfort
Commitment
Community
Compassion

Competence
Completion
Confidence
Connection
Consciousness
Conservation
Consistency
Control
Conversation
Cooperation
Courage
Craftiness
Creativity
Credibility
Curiosity
Daring
Decisiveness
Dependability
Depth
Determination
Discipline
Discovery
Diversity
Ease
Education
Efficiency
Empathy
Encouragement
Endurance
Energy
Entertainment
Enthusiasm
Environmentalism
Ethics
Excellence
Expansion
Experience
Expertise
Exploration
Expressiveness

Fairness
Faith
Fame
Family
Fascination
Fearlessness
Fierceness
Fitness
Flexibility
Freedom
Friendliness
Friendship
Frugality
Fun
Generosity
Giving
Grace
Gratitude
Grit
Growth
Guidance
Happiness
Harmony
Health
Heart
Helpfulness
Heroism
Honesty
Hopefulness
Hospitality
Humility
Humor
Imagination
Impact
Independence
Individuality
Influence
Ingenuity
Innovation
Inspiration

Integrity
Intelligence
Intimacy
Intuition
Inventiveness
Joy
Justice
Kindness
Leadership
Learning
Legacy
Liberation
Lightness
Logic
Longevity
Love
Loyalty
Luxury
Magic
Marriage
Mastery
Meaning
Meticulousness
Mindfulness
Moderation
Money
Motivation
Mystique
Openness
Opportunity
Optimism
Order
Organization
Originality
Patience
Passion
Peace
Perseverance
Persistence
Playfulness

Pleasure
Potency
Power
Practicality
Pragmatism
Precision
Preparedness
Presence
Proactivity
Professionalism
Prosperity
Rationality
Realism
Reason
Recognition
Reflection
Relaxation
Reliability
Reputation
Resilience
Resolution
Resourcefulness
Respect
Responsibility
Rest
Reverence
Romance
Sacredness
Satisfaction
Security
Self-reliance
Self-respect
Serenity
Service
Sexuality
Sharing
Significance
Silence
Simplicity
Sincerity

Skillfulness
Solidarity
Solitude
Sophistication
Spirituality
Spontaneity
Stability
Status
Strength
Structure
Success
Support
Teaching
Teamwork
Thoroughness
Thoughtfulness
Tradition
Tranquility
Transcendence
Trust
Truth
Understanding
Uniqueness
Unity
Usefulness
Utility
Variety
Victory
Virtue
Vision
Vitality
Volunteering
Warmth
Watchfulness
Wealth
Wholeheartedness
Winning
Wisdom
Wittiness
Wonder

ANYTHING NOT LISTED?
WRITE IN YOUR OWN:

Quality

Bosses are:

- DREAM CHASERS
- ADVENTURE SEEKERS
- HARD WORKERS
- CURIOUS
- LIFELONG LEARNERS
- WILLING TO BE WRONG
- HUMBLE
- UNAFRAID OF CHANGE

How does your negativity show up?

Being boss is about having a positive, confident mindset. But before we can talk about cultivating the good stuff, we must address what a not-so-positive mindset looks like. Sometimes a negative attitude shows up in sneaky ways. When these symptoms surface, you can be sure that at the root of it you've been hijacked by your own insecurities, fears, and negative thinking:

• BEING CONSISTENTLY LATE TO MEETINGS
• FORGETTING IMPORTANT INFORMATION
• NOT FOCUSING ON ONE TASK AT A TIME
• PLAYING THE VICTIM—EVERYTHING FEELS PERSONAL
• PLAYING THE BLAME GAME
• SHOWING IRRITABILITY AND IMPATIENCE WITH FRIENDS AND FAMILY
• ASSUMING THE WORST
• FEELING UNLUCKY
• FEELING THAT YOU'RE ALREADY TOO LUCKY TO WORK
  FOR ANYTHING MORE
• POKING AT LOVE HANDLES AND SCRUTINIZING PORES
• GETTING SICK ALL THE TIME
• PICKING FIGHTS

HOW DOES YOUR NEGATIVITY SHOW UP ON THE SLY?

FRAUDY FEELINGS

"So what do you do?"

This seemingly innocent question comes with a lot of baggage for those of us who are creative.

"Oh, I work as an administrative assistant, but I paint on the side."

"I am a designer, but I kind of write and sometimes take photos."

"I am too embarrassed to call myself a business coach, but I help creatives set up shop and believe in themselves."

The jobs we want come with big shoes, and to even begin to step into those big ol' shoes, much less our own power, brings on a shit-ton of fear and imposter syndrome. It's what we here at *Being Boss* call "fraudy feelings." Yes, sometimes we make up words and phrases like "fraudy feelings" because nothing else can entirely articulate that queasiness we get in the pit of our stomachs, the weight on our chests, the tightening in our shoulders, the knot in our throats, or the buzz in our heads when we have a vision that feels so much bigger and grander than our little selves.

If we were to say, "I'm an artist" or "I'm a creative director" or "I'm a business consultant" instead of beating around the bush or diminishing what we do with self-deprecation or deflection, we might get called out. If it's not our friend's friend, a spouse's colleague, or a distant aunt responding with a "And you make money doing that?" or "Oh. Huh," then it's your own inner critic rolling its eyes and saying, "You wish."

Sound familiar? That's because *everyone* suffers from fraudy feelings. Even the most successful creatives we've interviewed face big and little fears on the daily. The creatives you look up to freak out too—the only difference is they know how to go to battle. They know how to face their fear, see what it is, and cultivate the courage it takes to keep showing up and doing the work.

You might not know that you're experiencing fraudy feelings or imposter syndrome. Sometimes negative self-talk disguises itself as questions and comments from your own inner critic that pretend to be useful but are actually bringing you down:

• *Do you have what it takes?*

• *Why can't you be more like her?*

• *What will everybody think?*

• *You're lucky you even have a roof over your head. How dare you want to make a living doing that?*

• *If it's not perfect, then why bother? It better be all or nothing.*

• *You're too old (to learn how to dance; to pick up a paintbrush; to pursue a new career).*

• *You're too young (to be seen as credible or to call yourself an expert).*

• *You sound like a used car salesman.*

• *Who do you think you are?*

- *There's not enough room for everyone.*
- *Plus, so-and-so is already doing it so much better.*

DO ANY OF THESE RESONATE? HOW DO FRAUDY FEELINGS SHOW UP IN YOUR WORK AND LIFE?

CULTIVATING CONFIDENCE

Fear, insecurity, and self-doubt come with owning who you are, living and working your values, and being your own boss. Part of your job description is getting in regular staring contests with uncertainty—and you're not going to win every time. But here's the deal: when you sign up to be boss you sign up for all the scary stuff that comes with it. We have all lain awake at night wondering what we're doing, and we've all cried into our pillows wondering when it's going to get easier. You find success when you stop letting fear and bad vibes get you down. Those who are truly boss rise above, and in the face of their weaknesses and cracks in their self-esteem, they grab ahold of their confidence.

It can be tricky to define confidence; we want to be clear on what it's *not*. Confidence is not bending your own values or behavior to make other people happy. It's not about placing blame or playing the victim when things don't go your way, throwing a hissy fit, or always having to have the last word. In other words, being confident isn't the same thing as being an egotistical asshole. We're going to trust that you know the difference.

Confidence is standing in your truth and claiming your right to take up space and be happy even when your circumstances or feelings are a little shaky. Confidence is owning who you are and what you value, without apology. It's taking responsibility for your victories and mistakes alike. It's trusting yourself to figure out what's next, and having your own back along the way.

Cultivating confidence doesn't happen overnight—it's a hero's journey with lots of roadblocks that will test you along the way. But as long as you stay focused and determined, you'll begin to trust your strengths, work around your weaknesses, and keep your eye on the prize. You'll be able to take the next steps to get where you want to go even when you can't see what's around the bend. Confidence isn't a destination. It's a practice.

> *Confidence is a muscle. Just like we can develop strength, we can develop confidence.*

—CHALENE JOHNSON, *BEING BOSS*, EPISODE 20

What's on the other side of fraudy feelings and failure?

If you're feeling overwhelmed by your fear, just remember: all good stories come with a little conflict. Just think of your favorite movie—what kinds of trials and challenges did the hero have to overcome in order to make it to the happy ending? If you're struggling, high five! It means you're actually taking steps to clear your path, climb that mountain, and conquer your vision. Nobody ever said it was going to be easy, and besides, what fun would it be if it was? On the other side of your fear is everything you want and more.

Trust. Trust that you're smart. Trust that you're going to figure it out.

—DANIELLE KRYSA, *BEING BOSS,* **EPISODE 98**

Our friend and creative comrade Danielle Krysa started a blog in 2009 called *The Jealous Curator*—it was a place where she documented the contemporary art that made her, well, jealous. What started out as a place to hash out her feelings of envy has bloomed into a magical brand that has enabled Danielle to write multiple books, become a sought-after speaker, and—best of all—rekindle her own creative fire.

BEING BOSS: When have you felt like you failed, and how did you respond at the time?

DANIELLE KRYSA: I have failed plenty of times, but I don't really think of them as failures—those experiences are just bumps along my path. Granted, sometimes those bumps leave pretty

big bruises! One of the toughest experiences in my creative life happened only a few weeks before I finished my bachelor of fine arts degree. I was a painting major, but I really did not fit in at that school. I was used to defending myself in front of my painting professor and classmates, which, at the end of the day, is a pretty good skill to have. However, six weeks before graduation I showed my class the work for my final show. My teacher, who normally didn't like my work, loved these paintings! I was so excited—so excited, in fact, that when he asked for volunteers to show their work the following week in front of a visiting artist from New York, I put my hand up. How is this a failure, you ask? Wait for it . . . one week later I hung the same paintings I'd shown the Thursday before, but this time things didn't go so well. What was meant to be a ten-minute critique ended up lasting for thirty minutes, and in a strange twist, my professor and peers completely tore my work apart. I was stunned and suddenly my capability of defending myself was out the window. Close to the end of those thirty minutes my painting professor said, and I quote, "You should never paint again." Yes, that was a pretty big bruise.

BB: What was waiting for you on the other side of that failure?

DK: I allowed that experience to affect me much longer than it should have. I tried to keep painting for about a year after that, but I second-guessed every idea and every paint stroke.

Eventually, I just quit. That, to me, was failure. However, if it weren't for that critique, and the years that followed, I never would have found my way to where I am now. I wouldn't have been motivated to start my art blog, *The Jealous Curator*. I wouldn't have written books about creative blocks and inner critics being big jerks! I have a podcast, teach workshops, and speak all over the world. Why? Because I don't want anyone else to feel as alone as I did for all of those years. The only way you can truly fail is to quit. Don't quit.

BB: It's easy to see in hindsight how everything works out for a reason, but what advice would you give to someone who is caught in the grips of a creative block or their own inner critic?

DK: I think the most important thing to realize (and I wish I'd known this years ago) is that every creative person deals with blocks and self-doubt. Every. Creative. Person. Yes, even those people you idolize, who seem to have it all figured out. As soon as I realized I wasn't alone, that I was in fact experiencing the same thing as these people I admired so much, I was able to take a deep breath and cut myself some slack. I was suddenly in the same cool, creative club with these greats! Not a bad place to be, right? There is only one way for both blocks and inner critics to win—if you quit. By simply pushing forward, even on days when your pursuits feel like they're going nowhere, you are winning the battle.

After that terrible critique at the end of my BFA, I didn't push forward. I hid out. I didn't make my own work for years, probably because I was terrified of making something that wasn't perfect—so I just made nothing. Well, that was ridiculous. I've finally, and thankfully, come to understand that I can be creative every day without having to be a creative genius every day! The important thing is doing something that moves your creative life forward—that might be hitting the art store to keep your studio stocked, visiting an art opening with friends from your creative tribe so that all of you get a hit of inspiration (and free wine), or even puttering in your studio preparing bits and pieces for the next time inspiration strikes. Creativity is a lot like exercise—the more you do it, the better you feel, and suddenly you're living the life you want to be living.

Danielle Krysa has a BFA in fine arts and a post-graduate degree in graphic design. She is the writer and curator behind the contemporary online art site The Jealous Curator *(thejealouscurator.com). Danielle has hung shows in Washington, D.C., Los Angeles, San Francisco, and Toronto. In 2014 she published two books titled* Creative Block *and* Collage. *Her third book,* Your Inner Critic Is a Big Jerk *was released in fall 2016. Danielle has also had the great pleasure of speaking at TEDx, Pixar, Creative Mornings, CreativeLive, and Altitude Summit, and was interviewed for several video segments on Oprah.com.*

Confidence is a practice.

Often the people we consider to be fearless are just as scared as the rest of us, but what gives them a confident edge is that they know what they want and they have the courage to move through their fear. Here are some questions we like to ask people who exude an unshakable confidence. If you're feeling brave, go ahead and ask the most confident person you know some of these questions.

At the very least, use these as journaling prompts for yourself:

- WHAT DOES CONFIDENCE MEAN TO YOU?
- WHEN DO YOU FEEL MOST CONFIDENT?
- WHEN HAS YOUR CONFIDENCE BEEN SHAKEN?
- WHAT DID YOU DO TO OVERCOME IT?
- WHAT ARE YOUR CORE VALUES?
- AND HOW DO THOSE VALUES SUPPORT YOUR SELF-ESTEEM?

Inviting Beyoncé over for dinner

Enemies number one and two to being boss are insecurity and self-doubt—but they're something we all have to battle. A creative block, a piece of unkind criticism, and our own inner critic (the harshest of them all) can create cracks in our self-esteem and make our foundation feel shaky, rendering us unable to find our footing. So it doesn't come as a surprise that the question we get at *Being Boss* time and time again is **"How can I feel more confident?"**

Kathleen here. I often start my day by watching music videos—a habit that began in the 1990s when MTV still played music videos. These days, I have to turn to the Internet (Vevo, to be specific). This morning—like most mornings, to be honest—I chose Beyoncé. My Beyoncé crush started in 2003 when she was still in her girl group Destiny's Child but was venturing into a solo career. I was just twenty-one when "Crazy in Love" debuted—it was a Saturday afternoon, I was in my parents' living room watching the music video, mesmerized by Beyoncé. That booty. That belly chain. That unshakeable girl power. *That confidence.*

Over a decade later and it's clear "Crazy in Love" was just the beginning of who Beyoncé was to become. She's been crazy successful and graceful—and not by playing it safe or watering it down like most pop stars. She's a feminist, an advocate, and a change agent. She's not afraid to give oppression or haters the middle finger. *Boy, bye.* Beyoncé is not just an amazing singer and dancer—she's a creative director with a vision, a businesswoman with a plan, a wife, and a mom.

But even Beyoncé hasn't always been the confident powerhouse she is today. In fact, in 2008 she came out with an album titled *I Am Sasha Fierce.* Sasha Fierce was Beyoncé's alter ego. She was the persona who took over when Beyoncé was feeling nervous, had stage fright, or needed to cultivate her own booty-shaking courage. These days, Beyoncé is just Beyoncé. Through time, experience, and maturity she's been able to put Sasha Fierce to rest. Beyoncé no longer needs to compartmentalize the complex aspects of herself to have the courage to show up and be seen—whether that's as a business-woman who's boss, a sexy-as-hell performer, a mom with the same struggles as the rest of us, or a vulnerable wife.

So what do I do when I'm letting my own anxiety, insecurities, and self-doubt hijack my mindset? I invite Beyoncé over for dinner. I imagine that I'm inviting my own personal hero to the table. I offer her a drink (I imagine she'll take whiskey on the rocks) and a cheese plate with crackers, olives, and jam. We get a bit of small talk out of the way: "How are the kids? Are you spending most of your time in New York or L.A. these days?" Then we get down to business. I share all my deepest secrets, toughest decisions to be made, and most troubling concerns with Beyoncé. She sips her whiskey and I notice that her nails are immaculate. She really listens to what I'm saying and when I ask her, "So what do you think?" she tells me exactly what I need to hear. Depending on the day, she gives me no-bullshit advice, tough love, or a gentle "me too." I cultivate confidence by inviting Beyoncé over for dinner, asking her what she'd do, and then doing that.

Here is some of the advice I've received from my imaginary dinner parties with Queen Bey:

- DON'T BE AFRAID TO REDEFINE AND EMBRACE WHAT IT MEANS TO BE BOTH "FEMININE" AND A "FEMINIST."

- KNOW THE DIFFERENCE BETWEEN WHISKEY AND WHISKY.

- GET YOUR NAILS DONE.

- SPEAK WITH AN OPEN HEART AND WITHOUT APOLOGIES, NO MATTER THE COMPANY.

- DO NOT STAND FOR BULLYING—FROM YOURSELF OR OTHERS.

- FIND BEAUTY IN THE REAL AND IN THE PLACES YOU WOULD LEAST EXPECT IT.

- PERFECT IS BORING.

- TWIRL ON THEM HATERS AND ALWAYS STAY GRACIOUS.

- THE DETAILS MATTER.

- TAKE A DAY OFF.

- FOCUS ON YOUR CRAFT FIRST—THE MONEY WILL COME.

WHO ARE YOU INVITING OVER FOR DINNER?
WHAT KIND OF ADVICE ARE THEY GIVING YOU?

BE WHO YOU ARE 100 PERCENT OF THE TIME

There are industries that make millions (even billions!) of dollars by making you feel like less than the badass you are. *Buy these boyfriend jeans and you'll be a little more effortlessly cool. A little bit of Botox and eyelash extensions will make you look like you woke up like this. This shake will make your skin glow. This course will help you be more focused. These yoga leggings will hide your cellulite.* These industries, from beauty to information services and products, rely on your insecurities to make a profit. **You'll be more ____ if you buy this ____** (you fill in the blanks).

Don't get us wrong—a signature red on our lips decidedly makes us feel more bold and more boss. Fresh polish on our nails makes us feel more, well . . . polished. The difference is, we refuse to buy into hating ourselves *first* in order to invest in style or personal growth. We're not trying to mask our flaws but accentuate our fabulousness.

The most radical thing you can do for yourself in a world that is trying to capitalize on your imperfections is to love yourself—flaws, fabulousness, and all.

Keeping it real, committing to being who you are, and learning to be comfortable in your own skin are values we stand by. Being who you are means waking up every day and saying what you mean, getting curious about what you don't know, wearing what you want to wear, and expressing your truth. Owning who you are means that your thoughts reflect the values you hold true, the words that come out of your mouth are honest and contribute to the conversation you want to be having, and the actions you take reflect the person you want to be. Ultimately, owning it means you take responsibility for your circumstances.

Being who you are is:

- HAVING PRIDE IN YOUR STYLE

- SAYING WHAT YOU MEAN

- SHARING YOUR STORIES

- MAKING YOUR OWN RULES

- GIVING OTHERS PERMISSION TO LOVE (OR HATE) YOU
BUT, EITHER WAY,

- STANDING FIRM IN YOUR BELIEFS

- BEING ENTHUSIASTIC ABOUT WHAT YOU LIKE

EVERY DAY, YOU GET TO DECIDE WHO YOU WANT TO BE . . . AND WHO YOU ARE BECOMING. WHO DO YOU WANT TO BE? HOW CAN YOUR THOUGHTS, WORDS, TONE, STYLE, AND ACTIONS BETTER REPRESENT WHO YOU REALLY ARE?

CHOOSE ONE THING YOU LOVE ABOUT YOURSELF

Emily here. When I'm feeling too gloomy to think wonderfully kind things about myself, I head to yoga class. Not to get Zen or show the world how New Age I am, but because I'm very flexible, and that is my favorite thing about myself.

My physical flexibility doesn't make me a good business owner. It doesn't make me a better writer or designer or marketing planner. There's no way it's practically applicable to the life that I currently live, but it does make me feel really good about myself, especially when I can sink into my pigeon pose better than anyone else in class. Um, not that it's a competition.

Without fail, whenever I take time to notice the thing that I love most about myself, the gloom begins to dissipate and my confidence returns.

We can all find *one thing* that we love about ourselves. Whether it's your long legs, your ability to solve long math problems without breaking a sweat, or the way you lay hardwood flooring, make note of the thing that you love most about yourself and practice flaunting it (even just for yourself) when you're feeling down. It'll raise your confidence level and have you back to being boss in no time.

TRY THIS: WHAT DO YOU LOVE ABOUT YOURSELF? Start small. It can be a personality quirk you find endearing, or a physical trait you think is pretty fantastic. Now go big—what's that thing your friends can always rely on you for?

Love one thing about yourself and the rest will follow.
—BOB THE DRAG QUEEN

MAKE A MANTRA (AND REPEAT IT OVER AND OVER AGAIN)

When you hear the word "mantra," you might think of bendy yogis and very serious spiritual gurus. But mantras are for everyone, regardless of their ability to get into crow pose. A mantra is simply a phrase or word that you repeat over and over to yourself. If you don't like the word "mantra," you can replace it with "affirmation" or "focus." The best part is that mantras actually work! The repetition of your mantra carves out new neural pathways and makes new connections in your brain. So many of us have negative, limiting beliefs running on a loop—a mantra erases that destructive "tape" and lays down a new message, giving our minds somewhere more productive to go.

TRY THIS: CREATE A MANTRA AROUND THE VALUES YOU IDENTIFIED EARLIER IN THIS CHAPTER. For example, if your value is *freedom*, your mantra might be "I am free to make my own choices" or "I am free from expectations."

Some of our favorite mantras in work and life:

- I CAN DO HARD THINGS.
- THIS IS IT.
- DO THE WORK.
- I AM A MAGNET FOR DREAM CLIENTS WITH CASH.
- TAKE UP SPACE.
- BREATHE.

PRETEND AS IF

We've all heard the advice to "fake it until you make it." Now, in the name of authenticity, we don't wholeheartedly subscribe to faking anything, but we do think it's helpful to "pretend as if." Pretend as if every decision you make is the right one. Pretend as if you're the luckiest person you know. Pretend as if you're not scared of public speaking. Pretend as if you're perfectly comfortable talking about money or negotiating a contract. Pretend as if . . . and watch it become real.

WHERE HAVE YOU BEEN STRUGGLING? WHAT HAVE YOU BEEN PROCRASTINATING? HOW COULD YOU "PRETEND AS IF" TO MOVE FORWARD?

TURN ON YOUR TAXI LIGHT

Sometimes being comfortable and confident with who you are is as simple as turning on your taxi light. *Do what, now?* Hang with us here. Kathleen was once experiencing anxiety about attending a conference with a bunch of stylish, talented bloggers. As she fell into the comparison trap, being hijacked by her own fear, her life coach told her to walk into the room and turn on her taxi light. It's a tactic we've used ever since.

When you find yourself faced with a big room full of people, you don't need to hide your light in the corner or let fear keep you from the glorious encounters that await you. Pretend as if you literally have a taxi light on your head, pull the chain "on," and let the room know that you are open for business, or at least open to genuine conversations and meaningful connections. The visual of pulling the chain and turning on your light will trigger your mindset to shift from the negative feelings of anxiety to the positive opportunities that await you.

TRY THIS: TURN ON YOUR TAXI LIGHT! Try it first at the drive-through for coffee or in the grocery store while you're running errands. Notice how it changes your interactions with strangers and clerks. Keep practicing and try it at your next conference or meetup. Take note of how turning on your taxi light shifts your energy, thoughts, behavior, and conversations.

THE FEAR OF FAILURE

The fear of failure can be crippling to a creative looking to take any kind of leap, whether it is as big as leaving your day job or as small as creating your next work. This fear comes from not trusting yourself to make the right decision and can cause you to second-guess your wants, needs, and action plans to the point that you stand still, not moving forward for fear it will not produce the desired outcome. If you want to overcome your fear of failure, you have to get comfortable failing. Failing is a part of living.

In the world of being boss, you needn't be ashamed of failure. Success comes in time, and you should expect plenty of road bumps along the way. If you're doing the work, trying things out, and seeing what works, you're going to fail time and time again. It's part of the process of doing cool shit with your life, and that's how we know you're being boss. If you're not

Do not judge me by my successes. Judge me by how many times I fell and got back up.

—NELSON MANDELA

falling down, you're not trying to stand up. To help with this mindset, we reframe failures as lessons. This way we're not too scared to make a decision for fear of the outcome. Instead we make a choice and go along for the ride, because either way something good will come of it.

TRACK YOUR REJECTIONS

Along with tracking our goals—which we'll get into more in a later chapter—we make a practice of keeping score of how many rejections we receive. By making a game of it and seeing how many "nos" we can collect, we are more likely to put ourselves out there in the first place and less likely to take rejection personally, and we will inevitably score opportunities and big wins we wouldn't have had otherwise.

MAKING DECISIONS LIKE A BOSS

A product of fearing failure is the inability to make decisions, but being a decision-maker is at the core of being boss. Bosses trust themselves to follow the path of any decision. We figure it out along the way, and know that as long as we're making decisions based on our values rather than our fears, the path a decision leads us down is *our path*. This lends itself to some of the most interesting stories from successful folks, as they try out many opportunities, trust their instincts, and learn valuable lessons along the way—failed careers that nevertheless contribute to their expertise, chance encounters with influential people who help them along the way, unforeseen success that's far better than anything they ever imagined. Decision-making creates forward motion that will get you somewhere, which is often far better—or at least more interesting—than staying where you are right now.

We've found that most of the creatives who struggle with decision-making are choosing to bet against themselves, instead of betting on themselves. When you decide not to make a decision, either by pretending a choice isn't ahead of you, by staring at it anxiously for far too long, or by passing it off to someone else, you're betting that, if you were to make that decision, you would choose the wrong path. By not making a decision, you're choosing not to believe in yourself, which isn't very nice or productive. You're allowing yourself to be crippled by fear, and when that fear encourages you to give away your right to make your own decisions (which is the same as hiding from the decisions that are presented to you), you give away your power over your own life. If you want to be boss, you regain and practice your power to make decisions. It's one of the nicest things that you can do for yourself.

No matter how many mistakes you make or how slow your progress, you're still way ahead of everyone who isn't trying.
TONY ROBBINS

I don't like to gamble, but if there's one thing I'm willing to bet on, it's myself.
—BEYONCÉ

I have not failed. I've just found 10,000 ways that won't work.
—THOMAS EDISON

Pretend as if, every single day, every decision you make is the right decision.

TEST AND CHANGE

To help shift your mindset about making decisions, we encourage you to look at your life and work as a big experiment. We call it "test and change." The idea is to tackle every problem or opportunity as you would a science experiment.

In science experiments you're less worried about proving yourself right and more concerned with uncovering all the ways that you'll prove your hypothesis wrong, because with every failure you get closer and closer to success. When you don't get the desired outcome, you back up and try again, taking the lessons you've just learned and applying them to your next attempt. Test and change.

This method of working, making decisions, and navigating through life is much less paralyzing than being expected to get things right on your first try, and you're less attached to the outcome, leaving yourself open to enjoying the process.

Cultivating trust in your decisions stems from being kind and loving with yourself.

—**LINDSAY KLUGE,**
***BEING BOSS,* EPISODE 49**

YOLO (YOU ONLY LIVE ONCE.)

We're not trying to be morbid here, but the truth is, we're all going to die. When you remind yourself that you only live once (and according to our elders, life goes by all too swiftly), you can boldly live so as to honor your luck in being here in the first place. Nobody will be bragging about how much TV they watched or how awesome their employee benefits were on their deathbed.

TRY THIS: WHAT WOULD YOU DO IF YOU WEREN'T AFRAID?

WORST-CASE SCENARIO/BEST-CASE SCENARIO

When it comes to making a particularly difficult decision, we like to dig into the worst-case scenario and compare it to the best-case scenario. Here's how it works: when you're freaking out about an unsatisfied client, a rejection letter, a contract that fell through, or anything else that makes you anxious, think about the worst thing that could happen. Keep following this worst-case scenario until you hit rock bottom. Your worst-case scenario may end with you living out of your car with fourteen cats and a *Breaking Bad*-style drug addiction. But the truth is that *a lot* of failing with zero course correction would have to take place for this worst-case scenario to become reality. The worst-case scenario is usually just a bruised ego or hard lesson learned.

Whether you think you can or you can't, you are right.

—**HENRY FORD**

Now try imagining the best-case scenario. Instead of living in a van down by the river, you land a dream opportunity filled with first-class flights, adventures in the Alps, and green smoothies every morning for breakfast. It's all completely plausible if you do the work.

Imagine moving through life with the confidence that your best-case scenario is right around the corner, just waiting for you. It's natural to think

THE SCIENTIFIC METHOD FOR CREATIVES

Listen, we're creative entrepreneurs, but we're also science nerds. And if this method is good enough for cancer research, it's good enough for testing and changing any goals you have. Added bonus: using the scientific method will keep you from taking your efforts too personally.

MAKE AN OBSERVATION:

- I am not creatively fulfilled.
- I need more money to make my mortgage payment.
- I wish I had more Instagram followers.

ASK A QUESTION:

- Could pursuing art leave me creatively fulfilled?
- Will a marketing push get me more clients?
- Will using the same photo filter every time get me more Instagram followers?

FORM A HYPOTHESIS:

- Painting daily will make me feel happier and more content with my life and job.
- An email marketing campaign to my list of 1,000 subscribers will get me two clients.
- Posting photos using a consistent filter and cohesive color story will get me more Instagram followers.

CONDUCT AN EXPERIMENT:

- Spend two weeks rating your happiness on a scale of 1–10. Spend two weeks painting every day, rating your happiness on a scale of 1–10.
- Write and send out a email marketing campaign to your subscribers pitching your services for one week.
- Record the number of followers you currently have and then post one photo a day to your Instagram account using a consistent filter and cohesive color story for two weeks.

ANALYZE THE DATA AND DRAW A CONCLUSION:

- By analyzing my daily happiness score, I see that painting daily did make me feel happier. I will continue to paint daily.
- After completing the email marketing campaign, I secured one new client. Next time I will test sending a series of emails over a duration of two weeks.
- After consistently posting to Instagram using the same filter for two weeks, I gained forty-five new followers. I will continue using the same filter and cohesive color story, and pepper my Instagram feed with inspirational quotes to see if I can continue that growth.

See, we told you we were nerds.

NOW, WHAT EXPERIMENTS WOULD YOU LIKE TO CONDUCT?

	EXPERIMENT 1	EXPERIMENT 2	EXPERIMENT 3
MAKE AN OBSERVATION			
ASK A QUESTION			
FORM A HYPOTHESIS			
CONDUCT AN EXPERIMENT			
ANALYZE THE DATA AND DRAW A CONCLUSION			

of all that could go wrong, but what if you imagined, with all your senses, everything going right? What would your life look like?

TRY THIS: WHAT'S THE LAST THING YOU FREAKED OUT ABOUT? Money? Family drama? Criticism? Work? Take that circumstance and apply the worst-case scenario and best-case scenario to it. Take note of how those mindsets shift your reactions and behavior.

In order to carry a positive action, we must develop here a positive vision.

—DALAI LAMA

YOUR THOUGHTS BECOME THINGS

Your thoughts create your reality. That doesn't mean you can just think your way to being rich, successful, and famous, but you cannot deny that your thoughts create feelings, which motivate you to take action, which produces results that affect your original circumstances. Those new circumstances will lead to new thoughts. . . .

The beauty and the burden of your thoughts becoming things that show up in your physical world is that it's all up to you. What is it that you want? Do your thoughts help you get closer to your goals or move you further away?

The first step in changing your thoughts to something productive and helpful, as always, is to become aware of what you're thinking in the first place.

Meditation has made its way into mainstream conversation. Research on meditation is gaining traction and showing that everyone—from monks to CEOs—can benefit from quieting their minds. Meditation doesn't have to be complicated or fussy. You can certainly set the mood with candles, incense, and essential oils, but all you really need is your breath and your awareness. Meditation will help you get quiet so you can examine your thoughts, tap into your intuition, and get clear about what you want, what serves you, and what doesn't.

TRY THIS: MEDITATE FOR JUST FIVE MINUTES. Close your eyes and focus on your breathing. If your mind wanders, that's okay. Just keep practicing. You might also have better luck by following a guided meditation. We turn to the Headspace app when we can't find the motivation to meditate on our own.

THE COURAGE TO BE POSITIVE

It takes more courage to be enthusiastic about the things you like than it does to be cynical about the stuff you don't like.

Have you ever gotten together with a group of friends, only to bond over the things you don't like? Venting is important. It's good to know that we're not alone in our problems, but all too often what starts as venting and processing turns into unproductive stories about how everything sucks. We're not promoting a saccharine-sweet or Pollyanna attitude, where you pretend that life is puppies and rainbows when it's not, but an overly negative demeanor, all the freaking time, will cause unnecessary suffering that takes a toll on your relationships, your work, and your life.

Complaining is lazy. Gossip is easy. Oftentimes, it's easy for friends and colleagues to bond over what they don't like rather than be enthusiastic about what they love. Being positive and doing fun stuff requires a little more effort. So here are a few tips and tricks for focusing on the good and talking about the things you like:

• **Make a toast to the little victories you've accomplished in the past month.**

• **Share your favorite book, podcast, or television show with a friend.** Tell him why you love it and why you think he might like it too.

• **Share a helpful tip, trick, or tactic you've recently learned that makes work easier.**

• **Mail your favorite clients or creative peers a postcard with a love note on it.**

• **Be a tourist in your own city.** We know it sounds cheesy, but one of the best ways to get out of a rut with where you live is to seek out the best spots you might otherwise take for granted. When was the last time you visited a local art museum or went on a hike?

• **Send a friend an article that made you think of her.**

• **Challenge yourself to stop complaining.** Take notice of how much you complain. Then take note of what happens when you stop verbalizing every complaint. You'll be surprised how compulsive complaining can be, and how being accountable for your words will shift your attitude.

It takes more courage to be enthusiastic about the things you like than it does to be cynical about the stuff you don't like.

WHAT'S IN YOUR ORBIT?

It's all too easy to blame a negative attitude on circumstances or the people around you, but you're responsible for what's in your life. Playing the victim is not boss. Alternatively, pulling positive influences toward you and choosing positive thoughts will inevitably bring you positive experiences. This worksheet is designed to help you become accountable for whom and what you surround yourself with, good or bad. It will help you see how your thoughts and choices manifest themselves—from your career to your relationships to your home. What do you want in your orbit?

RELATIONSHIPS With whom do you spend the most time?

_____

_____

_____

_____

CAREER Describe your job in a nutshell.

_____

_____

_____

_____

OPPORTUNITIES Are you planning any special projects or adventures?

_____

_____

_____

_____

YOUR SPACES Describe the spaces where you live and work.

_____

_____

_____

_____

HOBBIES What are your favorite things to do?

_____

_____

_____

_____

First, fill in your core values at the center of your orbit.

Start labeling the "planets" with the people, projects, opportunities, and hobbies you fill your life with. Good or bad, the things you spend the most time and energy on will be closest to your "sun." Feel free to draw in more planets as needed.

Now that you can see the big picture, ask yourself these questions: Which planets don't align with your core values? What needs to fall out of orbit? What kinds of planets would you like to attract? Label anything you'd like to attract into your orbit off to the side of the solar system.

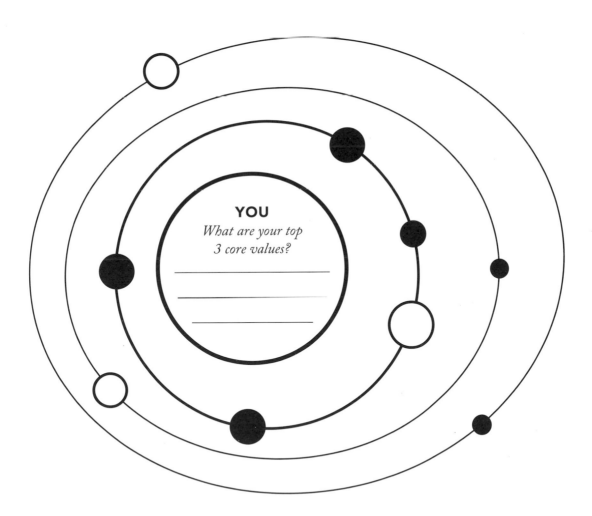

YOU

*What are your top
3 core values?*

Candle concentration

Kathleen here. Before I jumped into meditation I spent a few weeks developing my ability to concentrate and still my mind with this simple exercise in which I focus on a candle flame. To this day, if I find myself feeling particularly scattered or unable to focus during the day, I'll come back to this exercise to hone my ability to concentrate.

1. You'll need:
- a piece of paper,
- a pen or pencil,
- a timer, and
- a candle.

2. You'll want to sit at a table in a well-lit room. Make sure there aren't any drafts or open windows.

3. Get situated at the table, with the candle at least two feet in front of you. Light the candle and set your timer to ten minutes.

4. Now focus on the candle flame. When a thought pops into your head, make a mark on the piece of paper. Try not to take your eyes off the flame! And try to avoid moving any part of your body except to make the mark on your piece of paper.

5. Once a thought pops into your mind, gently let it pass, calm your mind, and keep going. You'll start out with lots of marks—maybe even hundreds! But the more you practice this exercise, the more you'll be able to focus on becoming one with the flame.

After doing this exercise regularly, I found that I was becoming even more aware of my thoughts throughout the day. I was surprised to find how often I was having negative or judgmental thoughts. I had no idea my inner dialogue was so full of complaints! This concentration exercise taught me not only to become aware of my thoughts, even the more subtle ones, but also that I have control over my thoughts. I started replacing negativity with optimism and kindness.

CREATE THE FEELING NOW

Anytime you are impatient for your next big dream to come true, try to experience the feeling of achieving the goal now. We could get a little woo-woo here and talk about how what you're seeking also seeks you, or how when you're vibrating at the frequency of the goals you want they'll find their way to you like a magnet—and we do believe those things to be true—but practically speaking, when you can create the feeling of achieving the success you want right now, you'll be much happier and confident in the process. Cultivating the feelings you think you'll have when you achieve your goal will shift how you behave in attaining those goals—making them come true with more swiftness and ease.

For example, let's say your goal is to launch an online course that makes you $100,000 in passive income every single year. Take a minute to close your eyes and imagine that you're already there. How will it feel to wake up in the morning to money pouring into your bank account? How will you behave? What will your conversations be like? Will it change your posture? When you reach this money goal, will it affect what opportunities you say "yes" to? Will you pitch yourself moving forward with confidence and clout? The idea is to get very, very clear on the details of how reaching your goal will make you feel and to begin mustering up those emotions and behaving like the boss you are in the here and now.

PRACTICE GRATITUDE

The truth is, you already have everything you need—self-love, creative expression, and confidence—and if you commit to practicing gratitude, you'll see that. There's no better way to cultivate positivity in your life than by paying attention to the positivity that's already there. Whether you wish to practice gratitude through daily prayers or meditation or by keeping a gratitude journal, focus more intently on the good in your life by making time to be grateful for what you have every single day.

TRY THIS: WRITE DOWN WHAT YOU'RE GRATEFUL FOR EVERY DAY. Keep a piece of paper or a stack of Post-it notes on your refrigerator or at your desk—a place where you won't forget about it. Before you begin your day (with your glass of OJ or before opening your inbox), write down three things you're grateful for. It can be *anything*, including your house, your friends, the cilantro on last night's tacos, or even a full night's sleep. Write them down in a simple list, and continue your day with your eyes open for what you can write down the next day.

Take a breath

Every year we go on a *Being Boss* vacation and invite seventy-five of our podcast listeners to come along. And every year we make sure to have our yogi friend Tisha Tate on hand. Her breath-work exercises not only bring us back to center but are the ultimate hangover cure when we've celebrated a bit too hard the night before. We wanted to be sure to share some of her wisdom and breathing tools with you too.

BEING BOSS: Hey, Tisha! You're one of those bosses who always seems to remain positive. What's your number one tactic for staying focused on the good stuff?

TISHA TATE: Take a deep breath. No, I'm not kidding—take a breath—right now. We sometimes hear those words as a tactic when a parent wants you to slow down or maybe during the course of an argument. But what does it mean to focus on your breath? Innately, it is both a voluntary and involuntary bodily function. But when you tune into the powerful tool you have right under your nose, you might be surprised by the benefits you experience.

Most researchers agree the average person takes between 20,000 and 30,000 breaths each day. Some yogic texts say we are born with an exact and immutable [number] of breaths for our lifetime. If true, then the longer each breath, the more time we get to hang out in this life experience. But if our journey is regularly plagued with stress, tension, and anxiety, we are not reveling in the pure joy and happiness that are available to each one of us.

Breath is the most immediate tool to move out of the sympathetic nervous system's fight-or-flight mode, which takes a huge toll on our bodies if we find ourselves remaining there for any length of time. The parasympathetic nervous system's "rest and digest" mode is the way to healing, balance, and general positivity. One conscious, focused breath can be the path to make the leap to the latter, where stress, tension, and anxiety are a distant memory.

BB: Breathing seems easy enough! Is there a specific kind of breathing exercise we can try to really bring ourselves back to the high-vibing boss we want to be?

TT: Let's try something now called a "square" or "box" breath. Before we begin, take inventory of how you feel in this moment. Where are you tight or holding? What's happening with your thoughts? Notice your breath. Now exhale deeply. Through your nose, inhale for a count of four. Hold that in-breath for a count of four. Again, through your nose, exhale for a count of four. When you get to the bottom of the exhale, hold without sipping any new air in for a count of four. Do that again at least two more times. I'll wait patiently.

Once again, take note of how you feel. What shifted? Is it even noticeable? The power of taking control of your breath leads to, without fail, numerous benefits such as heart rate decreasing, digestive enzymes being released, muscles relaxing, and many benefits beyond the physical. When our energy shifts and negative vibrations are replaced with ones of equanimity, our lives will spontaneously and without explanation be undergirded by peace and harmony, even when the wild winds of change appear. A deep knowing that "this too shall pass" without any weathering or scarring in your soul happens by simply and meaningfully tuning into your breath as often as you can.

Tisha Tate is a speaker and teacher who helps people slow down, let go, and come home to themselves through breath, movement, and inspiration. You can learn more about Tisha at www.tishatate.com.

**HERE IS OUR PERSONAL READING LIST OF
NO-BULLSHIT RESOURCES FOR A POSITIVE MINDSET:**

• *FINDING YOUR OWN NORTH STAR* BY MARTHA BECK

• *GIFTS OF IMPERFECTION AND DARING GREATLY* BY BRENÉ BROWN

• *BIG MAGIC* BY ELIZABETH GILBERT

• *ESSENTIALISM* BY GREG MCKEOWN

• *THE HAPPINESS ADVANTAGE* BY SHAWN ACHOR

• *SELF COACHING 101* BY BROOKE CASTILLO

• *PLAYING BIG* BY TARA MOHR

• *10% HAPPIER* BY DAN HARRIS

• *THE FOUR AGREEMENTS* BY DON MIGUEL RUIZ

• *LEAN INSIDE* BY JAY PRYOR

Being boss begins with a boss mindset and believing that you've got this.

• WHAT DO YOU VALUE?

• HOW ARE YOU GOING TO
CULTIVATE MORE CONFIDENCE?

• HOW ARE YOUR THOUGHTS
AFFECTING YOUR OUTER WORLD?

CHAPTER 3

ESTABLISHING BOSS BOUNDARIES

Being boss is knowing when and where to draw the line.

Most of the creatives we meet face a similar set of struggles: not enough time, not enough energy, not enough money to get it all done. If we all have the same struggles, then how do some people succeed while others spin their wheels? The answer is simple: the ones who succeed have set up healthy boundaries in their lives that help them discern where best to put their time, energy, and money—their most valuable resources.

Boundaries exist so that you can protect those resources—we'll be referring to these resources collectively as "energy" throughout the rest of this chapter. Without boundaries, you'll feel scattered and spread thin, eventually leading you to burnout, that place where the thing that once fulfilled you now makes you overwhelmed and disgruntled. You'll be taking client phone calls on the weekend when you should be nurturing relationships with your family. You'll find yourself with a calendar full of appointments that won't help you reach your goals. You will surround yourself with people who drain you instead of support you. You'll waste energy worrying about all the things that could go wrong. You will be paralyzed, not knowing what move to make next. Boundaries help you make decisions about how you work, who you hang out with, and what you do in your free time (including allowing yourself to have free time). Healthy boundaries help you determine when an opportunity will help you reach your vision of success. They help you decide what you say "yes" to and what you say "no" to.

Now, we know that part of the allure of being your own boss is throwing out all the rules and leading a free and boundless existence. That all sounds joyous in theory, but in practice there are few things less boss than an unfocused, undisciplined creative with no handle on what they want or how they're going to effectively go about getting it. The good news is that with boundaries, you will set yourself up to be a self-reliant and successful creative who's truly happy not only with the work you're creating, but also with the life that you're living.

The freedom that comes from being boss is that you get to set your own boundaries and make your own rules. By having boundaries, you'll feel like

Daring to set boundaries is about having the courage to love ourselves, even when we risk disappointing others.
—BRENÉ BROWN

you have your shit together, and you'll look like it too! You'll be the boss of your own time, not letting anyone or anything hijack your focus from the task at hand. You'll be the boss of your own energy, doing what you need to do to make sure you're in tip-top shape to accomplish your goals, and you'll find it easy to turn away people and opportunities that will deplete your reserves. You'll be the boss of your own money, knowing where it's going, the jobs it's doing, and how you will go about making more of it. When your boundaries are defined by you and no one else, you've accomplished the true freedom that being boss affords you.

But it's not just about the freedom to create the boundaries that you want. Working within limits also pushes creativity and innovation. Boundaries are important for the creative process—they give you the structure to focus on the tasks, people, and opportunities that will consistently and reliably direct you in creating your best work.

If you haven't revisited your boundaries in a while, then we invite you to do that, because otherwise you're unconsciously making decisions based on an outdated system of boundaries that may no longer resonate with you. You're automatically and mindlessly making decisions that aren't helping you be the person you currently want to be. That's not boss, and we'll help you redefine your boundaries on your own terms.

In this chapter, we will expand on your boss mindset to begin to establish boss practice, building boundaries that support the values discussed in Chapter 2 and making them real in your work and the parts of your life—like relationships, health, and hobbies—that are most important to you. By the end of this chapter, we want you to have a firm grasp on the parts of your life and work that need to be protected from "drains," and how to set up rules that you can take action on. You'll have your boundaries defined so that you can move forward with a comprehensive understanding of what you allow into your life, and what you don't.

Here are some warning signs that you might need to set some boundaries:
- You're not getting all of your work done and you see no light at the end of the tunnel.
- Coffee is your favorite meal of the day, and you'll go for another French press, please!
- Your calendar is so full of meetings and engagements that there's no time to actually do the creative work you love.
- You have no free time for self-care, hobbies, or quality time with family and friends.
- You leave social engagements feeling worse about yourself.
- Even when you're not working, your thoughts are consumed with work.
- The work you do doesn't fulfill or satisfy you.

• You're living paycheck-to-paycheck and always feel broke, or experience feast-or-famine money issues in your business.

• You find yourself saying "no" to the things you really want to do, like traveling or investing in learning something new.

• You find yourself being irritable and quick-tempered in your relationships.

• Your clients are texting you on the weekend (or texting you at all! WHAT!?).

ESTABLISHING YOUR BOUNDARIES: WHAT ARE YOU CULTIVATING? WHAT ARE YOU PROTECTING?

Boundaries are the lines we draw to contain what we want to cultivate and to protect what's important. Try to think of your boundaries as a fence around your garden. Having a clear boundary not only helps you focus your efforts and have a high impact in a concentrated area but also keeps out unwanted pests and critters.

Decide what you want to nourish and grow in your own garden, but also identify what fertilizes or nourishes your garden and what poses a potential threat to the things you're trying to keep safe. What goals, projects, intentions, and relationships do you want to tend to in your home, hobbies, and career?

In order to create boundaries that support who you are and what's important to you, you need to go back to what you value. In Chapter 2, you discovered the values that are most important to who you are; here we take those values and put them to work. Values alone are only ideas, but when you use them to guard your boundaries, you give them purpose—you allow your values to shape your life, to define where and how you spend your time, energy, and money.

You're also going to want to identify your energy boosts and drains. Think of energy boosts as fertilizer, sunshine, and water—the things that keep your garden healthy and thriving. Then consider your energy drains as the pests and critters that you need to protect your garden from—these are the things that leave you feeling depleted, tired, and overwhelmed.

Some examples of our energy boosts:

- SUNSHINE AND WATER. (IT TURNS OUT WE HAVE MORE IN COMMON WITH PLANTS THAN WE THOUGHT. SOAKING UP SOME VITAMIN D AND STAYING HYDRATED DOES MAGIC FOR OUR SOULS.)

- A FULL NIGHT'S SLEEP

- DINNER PARTIES AND GOOD CONVERSATION WITH LIKE-MINDED FRIENDS

- A GOOD, THOUGHT-PROVOKING BOOK

- TRAVEL AND ADVENTURE

- A GREEN SMOOTHIE

- DOING WORK WE LOVE

Some examples of energy drains:

- TOXIC RELATIONSHIPS
- TOO MUCH SOCIAL MEDIA
- ALL THE EMAILS
- OVERINDULGING IN REFINED SUGAR AND ALCOHOL
- WORKING EXCESSIVELY
- LOOKING AT A SCREEN ALL DAY
- GOSSIP AND NEGATIVITY

CREATING BOUNDARIES

Think of your life as a garden. What are you trying to cultivate and grow? How do you nurture your land and plants? How do you protect what you are creating from unwanted pests and critters? In each space of your garden, write in what you would like to cultivate and create in each area. These can be goals, intentions, values, or specific projects.

ENERGY BOOSTS

Make a list of things that give your life a little extra boost of energy. Think of these things as the sunshine and water for your garden.

_____   _____

_____   _____

_____   _____

_____   _____

_____   _____

_____   _____

_____   _____

_____   _____

ENERGY DRAINS

From weeds to pests and unwelcome creatures, what are the things in your life that drain your energy and resources? Make a list.

_____   _____

_____   _____

_____   _____

_____   _____

_____   _____

_____   _____

_____   _____

_____   _____

A NOTE ON WHITE SPACE

We left one square of your garden blank for a reason. It's always nice to leave a little space for an unexpected opportunity or something wild to grow. Homework: add some "white space" to your schedule. Can you carve out an hour a day, or a day a week, for white space?

CORE VALUES

_____   _____   _____

RELATIONSHIPS	WORK/CAREER	HOME/PLACE

EDUCATION/ GROWTH	MONEY	HOBBIES/FUN

EMOTIONAL/ SPIRITUAL	HEALTH	(WHITE SPACE)

CREATING WHITE SPACE

Emily here. We encourage you to create "white space" on your calendar, and for quite some time I have blocked off a single day in my week that no one can touch. This day is traditionally Thursday, and there are no meetings, no deadlines, *nothing*. It's a full day of white space that usually ends up being wildly productive, wonderfully rejuvenating, or somewhere in between, because I leave it open to accomplish whatever I need. Sometimes what I need to accomplish is a nap. Other times it's grocery shopping or catching up on some work. There have been Thursdays that included impromptu trips to the aquarium with my family, or a whole day in which I could dive into a creative passion project. Whatever I find myself doing during this time, it gives my brain space to be free, to wander wherever it will— allowing it to be playful. This white space creates a reliable boundary that gives me one day a week when my life and work have space to grow wild and free. I've found this space essential for my ongoing happiness in the job I've created for myself (a whole day of ultimate flexibility each week!) and also very important for my creative process. This day gives me a chance to *live*, which really helps me *create*.

WHEN TO SAY "YES" AND "NO"

As boundaries begin eliminating energy drains and creating more space for the activities that energize you, they will also define how you make decisions and take action, enabling you to use your time, money, and energy efficiently so that you take on only the opportunities, tasks, and relationships that align with what's important to you. When something aligns with your boundaries, it's an easy "yes." If it doesn't align with your boundaries, it's a "no." Your boundaries are the first layer of defense that safeguards your resources, giving you a structure for letting things into your life and also making decision-making significantly easier to tackle.

For example, let's say you get asked to join a board of a well-respected club or association in your field. You know it would look great on your résumé, be good for your reputation, and help you connect with your industry peers. The problem is that this opportunity requires regular meetings after the work hours you've set, cutting into time you've reserved for your family. Establishing exactly when you work and when you're available for your family makes it easier to say "no" to an opportunity that feels like it should be a "yes." This kind of decision can be one that produces a lot of anxiety, but it's easy to say "no" when you're clear on what you really, truly want. In this instance, saying "no" is easy because you know you're reserving your valuable time for what matters most to you. (Or maybe a redefining of your boundaries allows you to say, "yes!" Either way, look at the situation through the lens of your values to help you make the right decision.)

Now, you will still have to do things you don't want to do. For example, you might hate invoicing or keeping track of your books—but to be a responsible boss, you know you gotta do it. Try shifting your mindset to see how the task of bookkeeping supports your values and the higher goal you're trying to achieve. When you can see the big picture, it makes the daily tasks that much more meaningful and—dare we say—tolerable. When you can check off your to-do list without resenting the tasks at hand, you know you've got some good boundaries in place.

Using your values to define your boundaries gives you the reasons you need to choose what you want, feel confident in those reasons, and let go of what doesn't truly serve you without apology. Let your value-based boundaries guide your decisions, and you'll never have a reason to regret your choices.

CREATING PHYSICAL BOUNDARIES

Defining our boundaries can be physical as well as mental—we can also create literal boundaries in our work and life. Anyone who works from home knows the importance that boundaries play in getting in the zone and shutting it off at the end of the day, which is done by establishing a defined office or work area in our homes. Actions such as engaging our sense of smell by lighting a candle when it is time to work and blowing it out when the day is complete, closing the laptop and shutting the door to our home office at the end of the day, and turning the phone off (or at the very least shutting down notifications) on the weekends are just a few ways we create physical boundaries to establish a work-life balance.

BOUNDARIES TO PROTECT YOUR TIME, ENERGY, AND MONEY

We've all worried about not having enough time, energy, and money to do what we want to do. But here's some truth: worry is a form of procrastination and an excuse for not doing the work you need to do to protect what you have. With solid boundaries you'll find there's actually an abundance of everything you need to accomplish your goals.

Creating rules that make taking action and making decisions easy enforces and supports your boundaries. For example, if you create a boundary around your Saturday family time, then establishing the rule of "I will not check my email on the weekends" will support you in keeping that family time sacred.

Money and boundaries

Writer, blogger, and world traveler Sarah Von Bargen is brilliant when it comes to living the dream life we all crave. She's traveled the world, has great style, and lives in a super-cute place in the hip and trendy part of the greater Minneapolis–St. Paul area. The best part is that she's doing it on a very typical five-figure salary. How does she do it? She's created money boundaries that align how she spends with what makes her happy.

BEING BOSS: One thing we hear over and over again from creative entrepreneurs (and aspiring small business owners) is "I don't have enough money." What kind of mindset shift does it take to go from feeling broke to feeling like you have enough?

SARAH VON BARGEN: Feeling like you have enough starts with getting incredibly clear on what makes you happy. Most of us—myself included—have absorbed ideas about what happiness, success, and abundance "should" look like. Most of us subconsciously believe we'll be happier if we're thinner, live in a bigger house, are in a committed romantic relationship, and earn more money.

Some of those things are true for some of us, but it's very unlikely that all of us will be made happy by the same things.

When we can let go of those "should" ideas about happiness and get really, really clear on what makes us happy, it's easier to fill our lives with those happy-making things—no matter our income.

BB: Ah, so what we hear you saying is that a lack of money is often a blanket statement for being unhappy with what you have or even unsure of what you really want. If you can't be grateful for what you have now and you think money is the path to happiness, then you'll never be happy with what you have no matter how much money you make! The ultimate mindset shift that needs to happen to go from feeling broke to feeling like you have enough is to find happiness in what you already have.

So often money issues are a symptom of a deeper problem. What are some common money symptoms you see? And what do you think the deeper problem is?

SVB: One money symptom is making regrettable purchases. There are lots of reasons people make regrettable purchases, but two of the most common issues I see are:

1. Shopping instead of feeling our feelings

2. Confusing buying something with taking action

We buy a new laptop because we want to feel professionally accomplished. We buy a name-brand bag because we want to feel fancy. We buy a bunch of random stuff at Target because we had a hard day at work. There's nothing wrong with occasionally buying things to help us feel the way we want to feel, but shopping should not be our knee-jerk, go-to response for everything that ails us.

Many of us are also inclined to buy things instead of, ya know, doing stuff. Buying a bunch of new workout gear is not the same as working out. So many creatives buy ecourses and don't finish them. They buy a new camera lens when they don't really understand how to use the last camera lens they bought.

Many of us do this because buying for our business makes us feel professional and legitimate. Again, it's fine to do this occasionally, and having the right tools and software to run your business smoothly is important, but we can feel that same way by updating our LinkedIn account, updating our testimonial page, or just making some of those "I know I need to do this" changes to our website.

BB: *Amen!* **We see a lot of creative entrepreneurs buy into the idea that you have to "spend money to make money" and forget the whole taking-action-and-doing-the-work part. We also can't help but wonder if that maybe the deeper issue that is masked by our purchases is fear of showing up and doing the work.**

One of the things that you recommend to people is to "put their money where their happy is." What does that mean?

SVB: Very few of us consider whether our spending habits align with our happiness or values. You say that dancing makes you happy, but if you look at your bank statements, you'll see $0 going toward anything dance-related. You say travel makes you happy, but if you look at your credit card statement, you might see you've spent only $200 on travel in the last year.

Meanwhile, perhaps you're spending hundreds of dollars on fast food meals you don't really like, clothes you never wear, and books you haven't read. When you get really clear on what makes you happy and where your money is going, it's a lot easier to point your time, money, and energy in a happy-making direction.

BB: What are some money boundaries or habits you would recommend putting in place to be able to invest and spend on the things you prioritize?

SVB:

• If you share finances with someone, it's really, really important that you're able to have calm, loving, recurring conversations about your finances. Nail down which expenses you're splitting, who pays for what, and at what price point you need to "check in" with each other.

• Look through your bank statement and credit card statement at the end of every month. No, it's not sexy, but it's super-important! Make it more fun by clearing off the table, lighting a candle, ordering takeout, and pouring yourself a drink.

• Know how to respond when people question why you did (or didn't) buy something. People will question why you don't have a MacBook or why you need the latest iPhone. They'll question why you outsource so much or why you don't outsource at all.

My go-to response for questions like that: "It's just not a priority for me right now" or—as the case may be—"It's something that's a priority for me." Accompany this with direct eye contact, a smile, and a shrug. Then change the topic of conversation. Works like a charm!

Sarah Von Bargen is a blogger, writer, and teacher who helps people add more money and more happiness to their days and live their lives on purpose at www.yesandyes.org. When she's not on the Internet she's traveling, eating cheese, or trying to get her very patient husband to watch Friday Night Lights. *Again.*

FROM DAY JOB TO DREAM JOB

Let's bring the magnifying glass back to Carrie, the day-jobber-turned-photographer we introduced to you in the beginning of Chapter 2. We want to look closely at the transition period that came between quitting her day job and finding her footing in her creative business.

As Carrie quits her day job, she is elated by having her time and energy all to herself and her own endeavors. But, a few weeks into this newfound freedom, Carrie isn't feeling free at all. She's still working her usual schedule: still "clocking in" at the same time, still sliding through lunch at her desk, still feeling guilty about taking the time to practice her craft. Taking pictures doesn't *feel* like "work," so instead of doing the creative work she quit her job to pursue, she does the busywork that seems important but isn't aligned with what she wants to be doing all day. She's taken her old rules and definitions of what "work" *should* feel like and applied them to her new life, and they leave her unsatisfied.

This scenario isn't unique to Carrie. We've seen it happen time and time again with many creatives when they leave their day job to create their dream job—they hop from one to the other without adjusting their boundaries to support their new objectives. You're not here to clock in the hours, finish the task list, and scoot out as soon as 5 p.m. ticks by. Well, you are (your dream job is *still* a job), but it doesn't have to look like that; you get to make your own rules. You can decide that taking photos is more important than answering emails and that taking a full lunch break is more important than clocking in an eight-hour work day. *Make your own rules!*

The flip side of Carrie's scenario? When creatives quit their day jobs and let go of all old boundaries but don't bother setting up new ones. They begin sleeping too much, struggle with doing anything because they haven't identified what aspects of their life and work are important enough to cultivate and nurture, and let all of this mount into debilitating indecision and frustration. Soon the bills start to pile up and creativity dissipates with the resulting anxiety. It's not a pretty sight.

Without creating your own boundaries, you'll find yourself in a shit show. You'll either keep playing by someone else's rules—which are set up to give you an outcome that's not what you're here to achieve—or you'll crumble into a mess, with no direction or discipline. Setting boundaries and identifying rules is the first active step in embracing being your own boss.

And it's not just when you quit your day job and begin crafting your dream job that you'll be required to reassess your boundaries and rules. At every milestone of your journey, in your life and in your work, you'll be called to shift your perspective of what's important. You're required to *change* in order to grow.

*Entrepreneurs:
The only people who
work eighty-hour weeks
to avoid working
forty-hour weeks.*

—LORI GREINER, *SHARK TANK*

Imagine that you're creating an employee handbook for yourself.

- YOU WILL BE EXPECTED TO WORK ____ HOURS A WEEK. ANYTHING OVER ____ HOURS A WEEK WILL BE COMPENSATED EXTRA WITH ____.

- WORK HOURS ARE FROM ____ TO ____ AND NEVER _____.

- YOUR PAY IS $_____ / YEAR. YOU WILL RECEIVE A REVIEW EVERY ____ MONTHS AND WILL RECEIVE A PAY RAISE BASED ON _____.

- YOUR SELF-EMPLOYMENT BENEFITS INCLUDE _____, _____, AND _____.

- YOU DONATE ____PERCENT OF EACH PAYCHECK TO _____.

- YOUR COMPANY VALUES _____, _____, AND _____. THIS IS REFLECTED IN HOW YOU TREAT YOURSELF, YOUR CUSTOMERS, AND YOUR PEERS.
    - –DRESS CODE IS AS FOLLOWS:
    - –ON CASUAL DAYS YOU CAN WEAR _____.
    - –YOU FEEL MOST BOSS WHEN WEARING _____.
    - –ANYTHING ELSE? _____.

- YOU ARE REQUIRED TO TAKE AT LEAST _____ WEEKS OF VACATION PER YEAR.

- ON SICK DAYS YOU ARE EXPECTED TO _____.

As you're filling out this exercise, really consider the answers: Are these old expectations? Or are they honest answers that show how you would conduct work in the way that is most authentic to you? For example, in the past you may have been expected to come to work unless you have a doctor's note, but your new rules require you to take a bath and cuddle up with some Netflix. Maybe in the past you felt like tattoos and wild colors in your hair were "unprofessional"—now, what's your new dress code? What really, actually makes you feel most like your most confident self? Is there anything else you would add to your self-employment handbook?

NOW, IMAGINE WHAT A HANDBOOK FOR LIFE MIGHT LOOK LIKE. WHAT KINDS OF RULES AND BOUNDARIES WOULD YOU CREATE FOR YOUR HOME, FAMILY, FRIENDSHIPS, PHYSICAL HEALTH, SPIRITUALITY AND EMOTIONS, SELF-CARE, MONEY, HOBBIES, TRAVEL, FOOD, AND CREATIVITY?

Some of our life rules:

- READ TWO BOOKS A MONTH

- EAT YOUR FAVORITE MEAL AT LEAST ONCE A WEEK

- DON'T WAKE UP TO AN ALARM

- TAKE A RELAXING BATH AT LEAST ONCE A WEEK
(EXTRA CREDIT: ADD EPSOM SALTS AND BUBBLES)

- DON'T BITE YOUR NAILS

- HAVE SOME DARK CHOCOLATE EVERY DAMN DAY

- DO NOT READ OR SEND EMAILS ON EVENINGS OR WEEKENDS

- PUT CREATIVITY FIRST

- KEEP HIGH-VIBING AND SUPPORTIVE FRIENDS ONLY, PLEASE

- PRACTICE HEALTH CARE DAILY

- MAKE TIME FOR TWO HOURS PER WEEK OF INDULGENT SELF-CARE

- ALWAYS GET EIGHT HOURS OF SLEEP, WITHOUT EXCEPTION

- DELEGATE EVERYTHING THAT ISN'T YOUR CORE GENIUS

P.S. There are times when you break your own rules—
but you must have a rule in the first place.

STILL WORKING A DAY JOB

We know that not everyone who reads this book is already working for themselves, but that doesn't mean you can't create boundaries within your day job. We see far too many day-jobbers feeling that they must work sixty hours a week without extra compensation, they can't get that pixie cut or dye their hair pink, and they need to check email after hours, work while sick, and never take a vacation. These are self-imposed limitations, and you will never get what you don't ask for. If you can negotiate and set boundaries in the context of working for someone else right now, then it will be that much easier to do so when you're working for yourself full-time one day.

MAKING YOUR OWN RULES IN WORK AND LIFE

If you've ever worked for someone else and are Type A creatives like us, you probably read the employee handbook HR handed you on your first day from cover to cover. You made your way through training and orientation and knew exactly what was expected of you to get a gold star. But there is no handbook when you work for yourself—so it's up to you to create your own work policies and expectations (and, ahem, boundaries).

Let's talk about email for a second. Email is a great way to quickly communicate with potential customers, clients, and colleagues, but it can be a total time suck and energy drain, which is why you need to establish boundaries around managing your inbox. People expect you to check email constantly and reply immediately, and we don't like it. Constantly checking your email sets you up to react to others' needs, rather than be proactive in your own business and creativity. Being chained to your inbox is a hard habit to break, but we want to challenge you to chill on your email. Imagine checking your email only once a day and spending the rest of your time focused on your tasks and to-dos. (Sounds productive, doesn't it?) If this sounds impossible to you, it's probably all the more reason to practice getting some distance from your inbox. You might be thinking, "But what about all the people I'm going to piss off by not responding immediately!?" Listen, most of us aren't saving lives here. Plus, over time those who send you emails will begin to respect your boundaries and align their expectations to how you work best. We're not telling you exactly when and where you need to check your email, but we do suggest you figure out how to rule your inbox. Otherwise, it will rule you.

**YOUR INBOX, TEXT MESSAGES, AND SOCIAL MEDIA
CAN OFTEN OVERWHELM YOU. HERE ARE A FEW RULES
THAT WILL HELP KEEP SOLID BOUNDARIES IN PLAY:**

- YOU DON'T NEED TO RESPOND TO EVERYTHING.

- YOU DON'T HAVE TO RESPOND IMMEDIATELY.

- IT'S OKAY TO KEEP IT SHORT. THERE IS BEAUTY IN BREVITY.

- TURN OFF DISRUPTING NOTIFICATIONS—DON'T LET INSTAGRAM,
TWITTER, EMAIL, AND TEXTS HIJACK YOUR TIME. CHECK IN
AND REPLY WHEN IT'S RIGHT FOR YOU.

MANDATORY LAZY DAYS

A Mandatory Lazy Day is a day on which you are allowed to do absolutely nothing, as a way to cope with the stress of day-to-day life. As you hustle your job, family, social engagements, and responsibilities, it's important to lay it all down, sit down on the couch for a whole day, order in food or zap some leftovers, and allow yourself to just watch TV, scroll away on your phone, or stick your nose in a book. Unapologetically.

Emily here. We have a Mandatory Lazy Day in our house every two or three months, usually at particularly busy times in our lives. We set aside one day, usually on a weekend, when we commit to doing nothing productive. No emailing, no errands, no cooking (if possible). We keep our pajamas on, load up the Netflix queue, and just sit there. All day. We make as few decisions as possible, take naps if they call to us, and do whatever we want within the boundary of it not taking much effort to accomplish.

Though these days sound nice in theory, and we do find ourselves craving them, we usually find them pretty difficult to follow through with by late afternoon. We begin itching to *do something*, but we know how important it is to commit to this kind of rest. And that itch to do something is part of the magic. When you're living a boss life and running on full-blown passion and purpose, you have to take measures to recharge on the regular. You must find yourself back at that place where things are getting done not because they *have to* be done, but because you genuinely *want to* get them done. The thing that gets us back to that place is a Mandatory Lazy Day.

Here's how you have a Mandatory Lazy Day:

Pick a day in your not-so-far future that you can block off to be uninterrupted. I find that a weekend day usually works best. Label it "Mandatory Lazy Day" and let nothing and no one make their way into that day.

The day before your Mandatory Lazy Day, make sure you have easy food in your house. It can be leftovers, a simple salad, or frozen pizza for all I care. Make sure it will require minimal effort to prepare and put in your mouth.

On the morning of, stay in bed extra long. When you get up, don't bother getting out of your PJs. Make your coffee or tea, eat your easy breakfast—whatever you'd like, but do it slowly and with minimal effort.

Turn on the TV, open a book, or sink into an epic game of Tetris on your phone. Veg the eff out. Be unapologetically lazy.

Eat when you're hungry.

You're not allowed to:
- Turn on your computer or especially check your email.
- Leave your house (unless you need to take your dog for a leisurely walk—extra points if you do that in your PJs).
- Shower (unless you just really need to, but here's where a long, hot bath is extremely encouraged).
- Do anything that requires more than a little effort.
- Do anything overtly productive.
- Flake out and end it early—be lazy until bedtime and then go to bed. The world will be waiting for you tomorrow.

EXTRA BONUS POINTS: Turn off your phone the night before and leave it off until the morning after your Mandatory Lazy Day. With your phone off you will be less tempted to check your email, and you will have a full day without any outside input (except whatever book you're reading or show you're binging on). It becomes a full-world detox. Extra invigorating!

WHAT ELSE WOULD YOUR MANDATORY LAZY DAY INCLUDE? OPEN YOUR CALENDAR AND SCHEDULE YOUR NEXT LAZY DAY.

Success without sacrifice

Jenny Shih is a business coach who believes your career should support the life you want to live. When we had her on our podcast, she said, "Own what you want and refuse to give up what's most important to you." That resonated with us in a major way, along with her message to define success on your terms.

BEING BOSS: What is "success on your terms"?

JENNY SHIH: Success on your terms is a declaration of what you want to create both personally and professionally and what you're not willing to give up to make it happen.

There are no rules for defining success on your terms, and there is no right or wrong way to do it.

You can define success as achieving certain professional accolades or a particular status in your industry. Success could also be measured by a certain dollar figure, the number of people positively impacted by what you do, or any other quantifiable measurement.

The only thing to keep in mind is that YOU have to define it; no one can define it for you!

"Your terms" are simply the guidelines by which you want to achieve success. Another way to look at it is to consider what you're not willing to sacrifice to achieve success.

For example, I'm not willing to forgo sleep, eating healthy, or having quiet downtime on a daily basis. Others want time with their kids or to travel the world.

Another way to look at your terms would be considering what you value. Do you value health? Freedom? Time with family? Connection with others? New experiences? There are no right or wrong values, just those that are true to you. It's those values that will guide you in setting your terms.

Once you know what success you want to achieve and what your terms are, you then set yourself up to achieve that success without giving up what really matters to you. Put a different way, you're setting yourself up to achieve success in a holistic manner, honoring your professional aspirations and your personal desires.

BB: What advice would you give to someone who hasn't yet defined success? How do you actually go about figuring out what success on your terms looks like?

JS: If you haven't yet been able to define success on your terms, that's okay! Most of us are conditioned to think we should or shouldn't want certain things or that our life should or shouldn't look a particular way. The first thing we need to do is acknowledge what we've been conditioned to believe and give ourselves permission to figure out what is really true for us.

Once you've given yourself permission, the next thing to do is look underneath the conditioning. It's likely that you actually do know how you want to define success on your terms but that you've been afraid or hesitant to own it.

However, it could be possible that you really don't know what success on your terms means to you. If that's the case, the next step is to simply pay attention to how you spend your time on a daily basis and in the big picture of your life. As you do, notice if you're happy about how you spend your time or if negative feelings arise. Being aware of your time and your emotions will point you in the right direction.

For example, if you find yourself working late at night and feel frustrated that you're working late, that's great information! Or, if you take a Friday off and love that you took the day off, that's great information.

Whatever you notice is information that will help you figure out what matters most so you can define success for yourself.

Finally, it's okay to not know what success means to you or what your terms are. We all go through phases in life when we're changing from one set of values to another, and in those transition periods, we need to give ourselves permission to not know . . . and simply get curious.

BB: How does "success on your terms" help you prioritize, especially when you have a lot of things you want to accomplish and it all feels important, but you don't have the energy, time, or money to easily make it happen?

JS: The best part about defining success on your terms is that it gives you constant guidance on what to do when conflicts like this arise. When we've set our sights on something we want to accomplish but we don't have the energy, time, or money to make it happen, we need to check in with our definition of success and check in with our terms.

Sure, maybe we want to achieve that next big goal. But what is more important: being mindful of our energy expenditure or achieving that goal? Our definition of success on our terms will tell us whether we should back off on the goal or double down to make it happen. There is no one right answer, just the truth of what really matters to us.

If you reach a point where everything feels important and you've still bumped up against energy, time, or monetary constraints, it means it's time to further refine your values and priorities, and reassess what you really want from life.

Success on your terms doesn't mean you can always have it all. Success on your terms means you are being deliberate about what you want to create and how you want to create it. It means you're not willing to sacrifice what matters *most*.

Jenny Shih is an uncompromising business coach who works with smart entrepreneurs to start, grow, and streamline successful online businesses without having to work long hours or make huge sacrifices. Learn more about her at jennyshih.com.

COMMUNICATING YOUR BOUNDARIES

It's not enough to know your boundaries—you have to make sure the line you've drawn is clear to others, so that everyone is respectful and supportive of your choices when it comes to how you spend your time, money, and energy.

WRITE THEM DOWN: This first step will ensure that you're crystal clear about your boundaries to yourself. Write them down and leave them in a place where you can easily find them for future reference.

TALK THEM OUT: Once you've written your boundaries down, share them out loud with your people—whether that be your life partner, business partner, or peers. Let them know what they can expect from you, ask them if they have any questions, and reciprocate by asking them if they have any boundaries they'd like to explain to you. It's a two-way conversation and one that should be revisited quarterly because, again, as your business and life change, so will your boundaries.

ACTIONS SPEAK LOUDER THAN WORDS: One of the best ways to communicate a boundary is to respect them with your own actions. For example, if your boundary is to focus on your hobbies or family and to stop emailing on the weekends, then DON'T SEND EMAILS ON THE WEEKEND. It sounds obvious enough, but you'd be surprised at how many people set boundaries without actually respecting or practicing them themselves, and the people around you will take cues from you as to how sturdy your boundaries are. Don't say "yes" to things that don't nurture what you're trying to build; say "no" to things that distract you from what you really want to be doing all day.

MAKE THEM POLICY: One of the simplest ways to communicate important boundaries is to include them in places like the signature of your email, the footer of your website, or the bio area of your social media profile. For example, the most boss creatives we know include their email policies and hours in the signature of their email or even in an auto-responder letter so that recipients know when they can expect a reply.

DEFINE YOUR DREAM JOB

So many of us jump into creative entrepreneurship with big dreams of what our creative careers will look like, only to quickly get bogged down with all the tasks, to-dos, and hats we wear to get all the jobs done. When your life feels consumed by the not-so-dreamy daily grind, it's up to you to identify what you're best at and what you actually want to be doing all day, and then use that to define your dream job. This doesn't mean you won't have to continue to wear many hats, but it will give you clarity on what it is you want to be known for. This "job description" will act as a boundary to keep you centered in doing the work that you're best at and enjoy most, allowing you to decide what tasks you put on your to-do list and what you systemize or delegate to someone else.

TRY THIS: IF YOU COULD DO JUST ONE THING ALL DAY, WHAT WOULD IT BE? If you could quit doing one thing forever, what would go? Use the answers to these questions to begin writing out your dream job description and job title.

SCHEDULE EVERYTHING

The most common question we get is, how do we make time for all the stuff that we do? It's as simple as this: we put it in our calendar. If it doesn't get scheduled, it's not happening. From working out to writing to "white space," it's not only going on the calendar but is given the same importance as a client meeting or deadline.

TRY THIS: TAKE STOCK OF YOUR EXISTING MEETINGS AND APPOINTMENTS. Do they properly reflect your boundaries and values? Whether you use a paper planner or digital calendar, try scheduling everything that is "non-negotiable" (like your workouts or quality time with your kids). Layer in creative work time and meetings on top of that. Then live by your calendar.

THE POST-IT NOTE METHOD

As much as we preach the value of doing the work and pride ourselves on having the kind of work ethic and discipline it takes to be successful creative entrepreneurs, there are days when we feel sluggish when it comes to tackling an ever-growing to-do list. We do love our systems and use project management software daily, but when we really need to get moving, we turn to an old-school method for getting shit done: bust out a pen and a Post-it note. When your full to-do list is paralyzing your ability to accomplish anything, simply write three things on a Post-it note that you want to complete today.

More often than not, you'll get way more than three things done—but everything you manage to complete beyond the Post-it note is gravy. The note gives you the structure to accomplish just three things: write that newsletter, design that worksheet, and deliver on that deadline. Oftentimes, completing those three tasks will give you the confidence and momentum to keep going and tackle even more projects, but even if it doesn't, you can leave knowing you completed the three most important things on your list.

TRY THIS: WRITE THREE THINGS YOU WANT TO ACCOMPLISH ON A POST-IT NOTE. Be sure to break bigger tasks down into manageable to-dos. Cross things off the list as you go—there is truly nothing more satisfying.

LIST-MAKING MAGIC

By creating lists for yourself, you reduce the time you have to spend figuring out what to do next, because the answer is right in front of you on your lists! They hold your ideas, goals, and tasks so that you know exactly where to go and what to do when it's time to start working. We like having a notebook on our desk and a text file on our phones for keeping track of our lists.

WEEKLY TO-DO LIST: Once a week, create a long list of the things you need to accomplish that week. We oftentimes create this list on a Sunday night as a way to decompress from the ideas bumping around in our heads, to help us chill for those last few hours of *le* weekend, and to prepare for the week ahead.

DAILY TO-DO LIST: Check your weekly list and move the most important or time-sensitive items over to your list-of-the-day, queued up for completion. Do this each day of your week until your weekly to-do list is completed!

PROJECT TASK LIST: Any large project that needs to be completed, especially if it will take longer than a week, gets its own list. Write down every task from start to finish (don't worry about getting all of them; you'll remember more along the way), and divvy them up among your weekly lists. Then get to work!

MEAL AND GROCERY LIST: Bosses gotta eat. Meal planning and grocery shopping is something most of us must do! By creating a meal plan and grocery list each week, you define what you need and don't need to get at the grocery store, save yourself time because you're most likely to get everything in a single trip, and know exactly what you're going to eat for each meal in your week. It's the holy grail in saving you time, money, and energy.

WANT LIST: Want a new mattress, a replacement dining room chair, a new tool for your business? We all have wants, so why not keep a list? Our want list is filled with all the things that we desire but don't need to purchase in this moment. But when the time comes, it's easy to whip out our list and check off the next important thing! Or share it when it's time for gift-giving—your mom will thank you for finally being easy to buy for.

IDEA LIST: As a creative, you're never lacking for ideas! By capturing them on a list, you'll never have one slip away again. Keep a list of those brain nuggets in a little notebook that you carry with you, or on your smart phone for fast access. Then, when it's time to create, you'll have a bucket to access to get you started!

Your resources are limited—so it's up to you to draw the line around how you use your time, money, and energy.

- WHAT GIVES YOU ENERGY AND WHAT DRAINS IT?
- WHAT RULES DO YOU WANT TO CREATE FOR YOURSELF?
- WHAT RULES ARE OLD EXPECTATIONS THAT YOU NEED TO DITCH?
- HOW ARE YOU COMMUNICATING YOUR BOUNDARIES?

CHAPTER 4

HABITS AND ROUTINES

Being boss is a daily practice.

From the moment you open your eyes in the morning to how and when you decide to call it a night, being boss is part of your entire day. Your mindset and actions are constantly conspiring with you to move you closer to your goals and help you live a fulfilling life. You are the master of your own life. Every single day.

This "everyday" part is where habits and routines come in. While boundaries help you set some rules to nourish and protect certain areas of your life, habits and routines are the behaviors and actions that will actually lead you toward your goals. And when you practice them so much they become automatic, you begin heading where you want to go without even thinking about it. You start saving a ton of time because you're not considering every little step (like the first thing you need to do when you wake up in the morning), and you start working more efficiently and effectively (because the path is already laid out in front of you). We like to follow up on our rallying cry of "Do the work" with our unofficial motto, which is "Work smarter, not harder," and we do it by setting up habits and routines all over our lives and jobs that help us do just that.

If the backbone of discipline is boundaries, then habits and routines are how you implement those boundaries and actually *practice* discipline—so if you're craving more willpower and structure, what you really need is to practice good habits and routines. Because you don't need *more* willpower; you need those habits and routines to help you make it easy for you to do what you *will* to do. Habits and routines anchor you in your day and root you into your role as a creative entrepreneur. They're the antidote to the feelings of fear and uncertainty that plague us all.

In this chapter, we share how developing conscious and intentional habits and routines will support you along your path to achieving your goals, and—on the flip side—leaving bad habits unchecked will sabotage your success. We'll show you how to set up your daily boss practice by defining the habits and routines you wish to use to shape your life and lead you to success. We'll also introduce you to our favorite habits and routines, including goal and intention setting, and how these practices will create the foundation for taking meaningful action every day.

Fear and other bad habits

It's just as important to identify and break bad habits as it is to create and cultivate good habits. We're going to be focusing on how to set up the good habits that support your goals, but you're responsible for being mindful of the habits that keep you from moving forward. Some of the freedoms we indulge in, because we can, might turn into bad habits. Here are just a few bad habits we see:

- SPENDING TOO MUCH TIME ON SOCIAL MEDIA
- FOCUSING ON THE NEGATIVE
- PROCRASTINATING
- CHECKING AND RESPONDING TO EMAIL AFTER HOURS
- BUYING STUFF YOU DON'T NEED
- DISCOUNTING YOUR SERVICES OR PRODUCTS
- LETTING FEAR MAKE YOUR DECISIONS
- NEVER GETTING OUT OF YOUR PJS
- NOT SAYING WHAT YOU MEAN

WHAT ARE SOME OF YOUR BAD HABITS? DID ANY OF THOSE IN THE LIST ABOVE STRIKE A NERVE?

MAKING THE DAILY GRIND DREAMY

We all have this dream of what our days will look like when we're our own boss, but the reality is that there are still aspects of our jobs and careers that aren't so dreamy. The not-so-dreamy part of being a creative entrepreneur is what we call the daily grind. The daily grind is necessary and often what separates hobbyists from pros, but it can quickly hijack you from focusing on your creative genius to becoming reactive and getting caught up in the minutiae of running a business.

Here's what you might experience if you get lost in the daily grind:
- Feeling desperate for cash and clients
- Becoming reactive and unproductive
- Never leaving your house and feeling isolated
- Feeling unstructured—not knowing where to begin or what to do next
- Getting caught up in the details and ignoring your core genius
- Not having enough time to do what you really want to be doing

The goal isn't to get rid of the daily grind altogether, but to create routines to structure your day and help you balance running a business with leveraging your core genius so you're truly living the dream.

The best part of being your own boss is having the freedom to decide what your day looks like, from the first thing in the morning to the moment your head hits the pillow at night. The problem is that when the sky's the limit, you can feel aimless or unsure of what it is you're actually supposed to be doing all day. The weight of uncertainty, not to mention the never-ending to-do list, can paralyze your efforts.

Emily's morning routine:

- I WAKE UP AT 7 A.M., NATURALLY, WITHOUT AN ALARM CLOCK.

- I PICK UP A BOOK OR JOURNAL AND SPEND AN HOUR READING OR WRITING.

- AT 8 A.M. MY DAUGHTER LEAVES HER ROOM AND COMES IN TO TELL US GOOD MORNING.

- WE PROMPTLY GET OUT OF BED AND BEGIN MAKING BREAKFAST.

- AFTER BREAKFAST, WE GO FOR A WALK AND I GET READY FOR MY WORKDAY. (SOMETIMES THIS INVOLVES AN OUTFIT, HAIR, AND MAKEUP, AND SOMETIMES IT'S JUST BRUSHING MY TEETH AND PUTTING ON COZY SOCKS.)

- I HEAD INTO MY HOME OFFICE BETWEEN 9 A.M. AND 10 A.M. TO BEGIN MY DAY.

MORNING ROUTINE

How you start your morning sets the tone for the rest of your day. It's your job to set your day up for success, and if you're craving a bit of structure, your morning routine is a great place to start. Creative entrepreneurs desire process and routine as a way to avoid feeling lazy and uncertain. It's how you can happily marry the artist lifestyle with that of the entrepreneur. Plus, your dreamiest day will almost always start with your ideal morning, so set it up and watch the rest of your day more easily fall into place.

An effective morning routine is—by design—just the way you like it, setting you up to accomplish everything that needs to be done. It's your responsibility to take your morning routine into your own hands. In our experience, creative people crave a morning fueled by creativity.

When we ask creatives what an ideal morning looks like, we usually hear things like this:

• "I'd love to wake up with the sun in a fresh white room, in a fluffy bed with fresh sheets."

• "It would be super-dreamy to enjoy a cup of coffee on the porch—taking my time to slowly ease into my day."

• "I want to move my body! Something gentle like yoga or going on a walk would be ideal."

• "I'd love to make breakfast (either a smoothie or eggs)."

• "It would be nice to have time to read something inspiring—whether that's a blog, a magazine, or a compelling book."

• "Writing first thing in the morning—either pen to paper in my journal or busting out a blog post—would set me up for the rest of my day."

Nobody ever says, "I'd like to hit snooze eight times and then rush out the door with just enough time to pick up a burnt Starbucks before my 9 a.m. meeting, which will last until lunch—leaving my blood sugar and attitude a hot mess."

Take a look at your morning routine. Consider the following questions to figure out how to set up your morning for success.

• Take stock: How do you currently begin your day? What works? What doesn't?

• What are you doing in the morning that is NOT helpful or productive?

• What makes you feel energized and grounded in the mornings?

• How much time do you need for your ideal morning routine?

Now, begin to implement it. Maybe it will require you to wake up a bit earlier or just rearrange a few things in your schedule. Either way, claim the power you have over your daily life by creating a morning routine that sets up each and every day for success.

YOUR DREAM DAY

Imagine you are five years in the future—far enough ahead that the kinds of limits and attitudes that hold you back now are no longer in place. Anything is possible—you could be living on an island or waking up in a quaint cabin tucked away in a forest. Your money, relationships, and health are all in tip-top shape. Everything is damn near perfect. On the worksheet on pages 112 and 113, I want you to describe your dreamiest day in this world from beginning to end. Imagine that time is no object and you can fit as much or as little into your day as you'd like. Consider what you're feeling, tasting, smelling, touching, and seeing as you go through your day. Be mindful of how you want to feel, the rules and boundaries you want to live by, and the habits and routines you want to practice. Describe the events and encounters of this day in detail. Remember, this is a fantasy dream day—it's your story to write and up to you to design on your terms.

It's easy to let your self-limiting beliefs creep into place while you do this. If you find yourself saying, "well . . ." or "but . . ." or "that couldn't be because . . ." while doing this exercise, lighten up! Anything is possible here.

That being said, it's okay if your dream day isn't so fantastic. Maybe it's just a really great day at work that runs without a hitch. Or maybe it's the perfect weekend. The idea is to make it a day that feels dreamy to you on your terms.

GET IN THE HABIT OF TAKING CARE OF YOURSELF

We can't talk about developing habits that help you be boss without talking about treating your body, mind, and soul as if they are the most important assets of your business—because they are. Keeping your body and mind running in tip-top shape makes everything else in your work and life run more smoothly. If you don't feel well, you're not going to work well. What we're discussing in this chapter is frequently referred to as "self-care," but taking time to eat a nutritious meal, getting adequate sleep, and moving your body on a daily basis is not a luxury—it's a necessity. Good food, rest, and exercise are more than self-care—they're basic health care.

Once you start taking care of your physical health, it's enormous how much your mental health changes.

—MARIE FORLEO, BEING BOSS, EPISODE 111

LISTEN TO YOUR BODY

Disclaimer: we are not offering health advice here! We're positive you're boss enough to know your limits or check with a doctor if you're considering trying new things in your diet or exercise.

If you've ever been to a yoga class, you've heard the phrase "listen to your body." But if you're completely out of touch with your body, it can be hard to know what it's trying to tell you. Perhaps your body is telling you to eat cupcakes and wine every night for dinner, in which case listening to your body is the equivalent of listening to your wasted best friend at 4 a.m. who is able to convince you that bad ideas are somehow good. But listening to

If you really want to get your spirit and your soul and your mind and your creativity opened up to another level, you have got to get your physical body working on a daily basis.

—MARIE FORLEO, BEING BOSS, EPISODE 111

YOUR DREAM DAY

Describe your dream day from beginning to end. The trick is to get specific and imagine this day using all five senses—choose what you're feeling, tasting, smelling, touching, and seeing as you go through your day. But also, be mindful of your desired feelings and be specific about what you're actually doing. Think about the conversations you're having, the actions you're taking, and the things you're making. Remember, this is a fantasy—it's your story to write and can be as wildly improbable as you can imagine. Here are some questions to help get you started:

WHERE ARE YOU WHEN YOU WAKE UP? Think about location and bedding. Who's in the bed with you? What do you hear / smell / see?

_____

_____

DESCRIBE YOUR MORNING ROUTINE: Food / drink / reading / exercise / meditation / etc.

_____

_____

DESCRIBE YOUR DREAM WARDROBE: Pay special attention to your shoes—they reveal lots about who you are and what activities you love.

_____

_____

DESCRIBE YOUR ENVIRONMENT(S): Are you in a house? Co-working space? Out in nature? What's your favorite space to hang out in and why?

_____

_____

WHAT IS YOUR DAY LIKE? Conversations / actions / food / meetings / music / creating and making / blogging / writing. How do you feel?

_____

_____

WHAT FILLS YOUR EVENINGS? Food / drink / lighting / exercise / TV / people.

_____

_____

This is space in which you can brainstorm and organize your ideal day. Use it how you see fit.

MORNING:

_____

_____

_____

_____

_____

_____

AFTERNOON:

_____

_____

_____

_____

_____

_____

EVENING:

_____

_____

_____

_____

_____

_____

COMMIT TO ONE THING FOR THE NEXT FOUR DAYS: Pick one element of this ideal day and start incorporating it into your present-day reality for the next four days.

_____

HOMEWORK ASSIGNMENT: Start a Pinterest board to capture the look and feel of your ideal day. Think home / food / nature / travel / people / wardrobe / work / etc.

Now that you've gone through the exercise, let's reflect on your dream day:
- How is your dream day different from your current reality? How is it the same?
- Does your dream day include work? If so, what kind of work are you doing? If it doesn't include work, why?
- What would be the biggest change that would have to happen in order for your dream day to be a reality? Would you need to move? Would you need to change jobs or your entire career?
- Is your dream day dependent on another person showing up in (or even leaving) your life?
- What is the smallest change you could make in order to make your dream day a reality?

Commit to making one small element of your dream day a reality for the next four days. We're not asking you to overhaul your way of being or to undertake a huge lifestyle change; just give yourself four solid days to commit to one small change and see how it feels. The trick lies in keeping it as small as possible (radical overhauls are hard to stick to—we've all seen how this pans out with New Year's resolutions). If this new habit makes you feel good, don't stop at four days—keep going!

The more specific you are as you go through this exercise, the easier it will be to know what your dream day truly looks like. The more clearly you can see your dream day, the closer it is to becoming a reality for you. If you're vague or having a hard time connecting to your dream day, here are a few more tactics that can help:

Imagine a day in the life of someone who makes you green with envy. You know the one—the person you see on Instagram and who makes you think "Ugh. Her life is PERFECT." What do you imagine happening in this person's daily life that you're so jealous of? That can be a clue to your own desires and needs. Try to be especially imaginative and take a look at how the object of your envy actually *behaves*. Is she more spiritual because she takes time to meditate? Does she get more clients because she is consistent with content? Is she always celebrating victories and launches with champagne? Try behaving like the person who has you all in a tizzy and see what happens in your own life.

Create a physical mood board. An old-school way to do this is to bust out some poster board, glue sticks, and a stack of magazines that inspire you. Cut out images and words that encapsulate what you truly want. You can also curate a board on Pinterest or simply create a folder on your computer where you save images that inspire your dream day. A mood board will help bring texture, visuals, and focus to the life you want to design.

Remember, you are the boss of your life. Taking the time to practice new habits is how you proactively design and really begin living your dream day, every day.

your body can be as simple as recognizing the link between being stressed out and coming down with a cold. It's knowing how emotions physically manifest themselves in your body, and letting gut feelings (or the feelings that show up anywhere else) be a part of your decision-making process.

Here are some tactics that have helped us become more confident in listening to our bodies:

A sugar detox: Clearing our systems of added and refined sugar helps us better understand our cravings, and how sugar might not be the best fuel for being boss.

Yoga or weight lifting: Any kind of exercise that puts an emphasis on mind-body connection will help you learn how to mentally process what you're feeling in your physical body.

Meditation: Taking time every day, whether that's thirty minutes or a single moment, to be mindful of your breath is a great way to tune in and bring energy to your work and life.

EAT REAL FOOD

It should be a no-brainer that eating whole, unprocessed foods, mostly including ethically sourced meats, organic vegetables, eggs, fruits, nuts, and seeds, is the best way to reduce inflammation, get better sleep, boost self-esteem and confidence, and find your way out of brain fog. We know that eating real food makes us feel better, but it's all too easy to reach for sugary treats and processed food because it's convenient. Making good food a conscious, intentional habit will help you be more boss.

If the idea of giving up cheese or your nightly glass of wine makes you want to burn this book, here are a few small ideas you can try:

Eat more greens: You don't have to eliminate anything from your diet. Just challenge yourself to eat greens with each meal.

Stay hydrated: If you're feeling foggy or agitated, it's likely you're simply dehydrated. Aim for eight glasses of water a day or half your body weight in ounces—more if you exercise or it's hot outside.

Drink herbal tea: Mindfully sipping a cup of *tulsi*, also known as holy basil (or any other kind of herbal tea), when you're feeling anxious or upset will help you chill out.

To be a really successful entrepreneur, the first person you have to take care of is yourself.

—MELISSA HARTWIG, CO-CREATOR OF THE WHOLE30, AUTHOR OF *FOOD FREEDOM FOREVER, BEING BOSS,* EPISODE 91

GET ENOUGH SLEEP

At some point, sacrificing sleep to do the work became a badge of honor among creatives and working professionals—but cashing in your z's in the name of productivity is anything but boss. Sleep experts recommend you get at least eight hours of sleep a night in order to function at the top of your game—as if you need to be reminded. However, it's easy to fall into the bad habit of sacrificing sleep. Sleep is not a luxury—it's a necessity.

Some tips to help you sleep like a boss:

If you really want to be at the top of your game, you cannot allow yourself to sacrifice sleep.

—CHRISTINE HANSEN, SLEEP COACH, *BEING BOSS,* EPISODE 80

Set a nighttime alarm that reminds you to go to bed, just as you would a morning alarm for waking up. Simple, but genius!

Limit screens for at least an hour before settling into bed. The blue light emitted by your tech can trick your body into thinking it's still daytime.

Don't read about business right before bed! Save the books that will get your gears turning for your morning routine.

Wake up at the same time every day, even on the weekends! You don't have to be a member of the "5 a.m. club" to be a boss. If you like to sleep in, own it every day!

Create a nighttime routine. Just as a morning routine helps you wake up, doing the same thing every night will help your brain unwind and know it's time to catch some sweet, sweet z's.

BE KIND TO YOURSELF

As overachieving Type A creatives who often suffer from perfectionism-itis, we can be really hard on ourselves, and that's putting it mildly. So here's your reminder, in case you need it: be nice to yourself. All you can do is your own personal best any given day. Here are a few key things we've learned about having our own backs:

All of your power is within your thinking.

—**BROOKE CASTILLO, LIFE COACH,** *BEING BOSS,* **EPISODE 25**

Your word is your wand: This bit of wisdom comes from metaphysician Florence Scovel Shinn. The idea is that the things you say out loud (or think to yourself, really) will become your reality. If you want to manifest a productive and creative reality, say and think productive and creative things.

What would your best friend say? It's easy to be hard on ourselves, but imagine that you were your own best friend. What would she say about the thing you're beating yourself up about?

Give yourself ninety seconds to feel bad: So often we're obsessed with feeling good all the time, but what if we allowed ourselves to fully feel shitty, sad, or scared in the moment? If you'll give yourself even just ninety seconds to fully embrace your emotions, you will be able to get over them and get on with it much quicker than if you bottle them up inside.

If you need a refresher on the importance of being kind to yourself, we suggest you head back to Chapter 2, where we cover all the bases when it comes to the importance of positive thinking.

HERE ARE SOME OF OUR HABITS AND ROUTINES THAT MAKE OUR DAILY GRIND A LITTLE MORE DREAMY:

- SET UP TWO LUNCH DATES A MONTH WITH FRIENDS

- DO YOGA EVERY WEEK DURING BUSINESS HOURS

- STOCK UP ON SALADS AND PREP YOUR MEALS FOR THE WEEK

- START THE DAY WHEN YOU FEEL LIKE IT

- TAKE A DAILY WALK

- HAVE A GREEN SMOOTHIE

- WORK FROM A COFFEE SHOP, YOUR KITCHEN TABLE, OR BY A POOL

- MAKE SURE YOU HAVE NON-WORK-RELATED CONVERSATIONS DAILY

Self-care vs. health care

Health coach and acupuncturist Amy Kuretsky is our good friend and go-to boss when we have questions about taking care of our bodies, minds, and spirits.

BEING BOSS: **What's the difference between self-care and health care?**

AMY KURETSKY: Self-care treats more than just the body—it's purposeful and preventable care of the whole self: mind, body, and spirit.

Health care is what keeps you alive, but self-care is what allows you to really live. I know that sounds like a big, crazy statement, but I honestly find it true for myself and many of my clients.

You could go through the motions of your health care every day (things like brushing your teeth, taking your vitamins, eating nutritious food, moving your body, and getting adequate sleep) and still feel like something is lacking. It's only when you incorporate elements of self-care (things like spending time in nature, quieting your mind through meditation, and incorporating elements of fun into your day) that you feel inspired to create the type of business and life you want.

BB: **How does taking care of your health fuel your hustle?**

AK: One of the most obvious ways I see it manifesting is through my inputs and outputs. When I consume a bunch of crap (things like junk food, too much social media, and negative news reports), my motivation and creativity totally tank and the content I create suffers as a result.

But when I consume foods, words, and ideas that vibrate at a higher frequency (things like fresh and nutritious food, positive support from friends, books on expanding my awareness), I literally start to vibe higher, and I'm able to create some of my best content—the type of content that resonates with and attracts my dreamiest clients.

I also see the connection on a quieter level, too. Like many of my clients, I have a lot of voices in my head telling me what I should and shouldn't do. There's the voice of my inner critic, the voices of expert authors and podcast hosts, the voices of successful bosses I look up to. The list is endless, but somewhere in that sea of voices lies my voice. It can be hard to hear my voice sometimes, but when I commit to a daily mindfulness practice, I'm more able to quiet down the noise and tune into my own voice more clearly. Tapping into that voice—my intuition—empowers me to run my business in a way that's aligned with my truth and ends up attracting more of my dream clients, mentors, and collaborators.

And lastly, when I wake up early to work out in the morning (like 6 a.m.), I'm ten times more productive. I can't really even explain why—it's just a thing that always happens and I'm more than happy to go with it.

BB: What do you tell a creative entrepreneur when things like time and money feel like barriers to proper health care?

AK: If your barrier is time and your business is based upon your creativity, then you can't afford *not* to make time for self-care. Think about the last time you came up with a *really big idea*. I bet that it didn't happen during your scheduled work hours with your eyes glued to your laptop. You probably struck gold while going for a walk, taking a shower, or after a nice long nap. Our brains don't like feeling like caged animals—they are at their most creative when we let them out to play!

If your barrier is money, know that self-care doesn't have to look like weekly appointments with the acupuncturist or week-long trips to a spa. Self-care can be as simple and cheap as crafting a morning routine that makes you feel inspired, cared for, and energized. The only thing holding you back from creating a self-care routine within your budget is your own beliefs around what self-care is supposed to look like.

BB: What kinds of non-negotiable health-care routines would you recommend to a creative entrepreneur?

AK: Don't trade sleep for work. Ever. I get that sometimes you feel that you need to pull an all-nighter in order to get work done in time, but starting down that path is a slippery slope. Sleep is a necessary break for our body to do much-needed cleanup work. It's during this time that our brains are able to form new connections and pathways, as well as get rid of old data. This deep clean helps us solidify any new learning and makes the much-needed space for new creative thoughts to arise.

The other non-negotiable routine is to move your body daily. If you tend to be exercise-adverse, please note that I'm not talking about regular marathon training or high-intensity workouts (though, if that's your thing, do it!)—I'm talking about any activity that gets you up and moving a couple times a day. It could be a simple walk around the neighborhood with your dog, a couple minutes of stretching first thing in the morning, or even a short cleaning session to tidy up your home or office at the end of your workday. When we move our bodies, we move our energy. And the number one way to keep your creativity flowing and avoid feeling "stuck" in your creative work is to keep your energy flowing in your body by moving your body.

Amy Kuretsky is a health coach and acupuncturist working in Minneapolis, Minnesota, and at www.amykuretsky.com. Her passion is helping creative entrepreneurs become their healthiest selves without sacrificing their love of the hustle in the process. She wholeheartedly believes that only one person knows what's best for you (that's you!), and her work as a coach is all about helping you better tap into that inner wisdom and find your own unique brand of work–life balance.

A tea ritual

One of our favorite rituals is taking the time to sip a hot cup of herbal tea. Not only does it bring us back to center and reminds us to be present, but also the herbs themselves can be beneficial for our minds and bodies on a physiological level! We asked our herbalist friend Lindsay Kluge to tell us about her favorite herbal teas that can be found at any health-food store.

TO ENCOURAGE CREATIVITY: Damiana (*Turnera diffusa*), 1 tsp steeped in 2 cups hot water for a peppery, vibrant, creatively stimulating daily tonic.

TO ENHANCE FOCUS: Lemon balm tea from Traditional Medicinals

TO UPLIFT THE MOOD: Organic India Tulsi tea (holy basil) is like a "hug in a cup."

TO CALM THE MIND AND BODY: Simple chamomile and peppermint tea to relax the central nervous system and bring awareness to your senses. Steep ½ tsp each in 2 cups hot water, for 10 minutes. Sip consciously throughout the day.

Lindsay Kluge, MSc, is a clinical herbalist and licensed dietitian nutritionist in Richmond, Virginia. She has created a clinical practice that incorporates botanical medicines, Ayurvedic and holistic nutrition, and joyful eating to help people establish a balance of health and happiness. Learn more at www.gingertonicbotanicals.com.

BEING A BALANCED BOSS

Here's an exercise that will help you identify which habits drain your energy and which ones support a healthy body and mind. This worksheet will help you to see how you might change your behavior or modify your habits to be a more balanced boss.

I think we can all agree that the work-life balance is a bit of a myth. But we think there is something to be said for taking stock of where you are in all areas of life so you can at least feel a little more . . . well, balanced. The goal of this worksheet is to see which habits give you energy in different aspects of your life, and to put together an action plan for the areas that could use a little more attention.

PHYSICAL HABITS

When do you feel physically healthy and most alive?

_____

_____

_____

What kinds of foods make you feel nourished?

_____

_____

_____

_____

What's the most luxurious thing you like to do for your body?

_____

_____

_____

What makes you feel physically drained?

_____

_____

_____

_____

MENTAL HABITS

What is your favorite headspace to be in?

_____

_____

_____

_____

What are you typically doing when you're in "the zone"?

_____

_____

_____

_____

What is your favorite thing to learn more about / read / consume?

_____

_____

_____

What makes you feel most mentally fatigued?

_____

_____

_____

_____

To be a really successful entrepreneur, the first person you have to take care of is yourself.

—MELISSA HARTWIG, "BUILDING THE WHOLE30 EMPIRE,"
BEING BOSS, EPISODE 34

EMOTIONAL HABITS

When do you feel the most connection or love?

_____

_____

_____

_____

Describe the emotions you want to feel most often as you move through life:

_____

_____

_____

_____

Describe how you behave when you feel good:

_____

_____

_____

_____

What makes you feel emotionally exhausted?

_____

_____

_____

_____

THE ACTION PLAN

Looking at your answers above, pick just one thing in each section you will add to (or omit from) your life. Think about making these habits little things you can execute each day, or if that's not possible, at least schedule them on your calendar weekly, monthly, or yearly.

PHYSICAL:

I will do _____.

I will stop doing _____.

MENTAL:

I will do _____.

I will stop doing _____.

EMOTIONAL:

I will do _____.

I will stop doing _____.

SETTING GOALS LIKE A BOSS

The most successful people that we know regularly set goals that help them define success and create the reality they want. When you are working for yourself, you are the only person holding yourself accountable. Period. And you will never feel more boss than when you've set a big *makes-you-want-to-throw-up* goal for yourself and actually reach it. Be warned: that feeling can be addicting, but fortunately, continually setting the bar high for yourself isn't a bad habit to form.

In order to find success, which is the result of reaching your goals, you have to get really specific about what your goals actually look and feel like—and then you must make space for them. If you don't have a place to track exactly what you want, you'll constantly be moving the bar higher and wanting more, without ever celebrating how far you've come. You'll feel that you're never enough.

Before we get much further, let's talk about what makes a goal "good." Too often we'll see creatives setting vague benchmarks for themselves, such as "I want to quit my day job" or "I want financial freedom" or "I'd love to have a ton of clients." These are all wonderful ideas—but we need to get a little more specific when setting a goal. What will it take to quit that day job? What exactly does "financial freedom" mean? How many clients is a ton of clients? And what are those clients like?

A GOOD GOAL IS:

Specific. Keep boiling down your goal until it becomes super-specific and leaves no question in mind as to exactly what you want.

Measurable. If you're basing your goal on a feeling, it's too vague. Your goal should be measurable so that you can always check in on your progress and how much further you have to go.

Actionable. If you can't break your goal down into action steps, it may not be specific enough to actually attain.

Rewarding. The process of working toward your goal should feel as good as the actual achievement at the end of the road.

Timed. By what day, week, month, or year do you want to achieve your goal? Setting a time limit will put a little hustle in your bustle. (However, sometimes the path to big ass goals is a little winding, so don't prematurely ditch your goal if you haven't achieved it within your designated time frame.)

Your goals, minus your doubts, equal your reality.

—RALPH MARSTON

The Chalkboard Method®

Kathleen here. When I launched my business, Braid Creative, I spent months getting my branding, website, social media, and blog posts together. My closest friends and family were super-excited about my new creative endeavor, but once the launch frenzy died down and the dust had settled, I found myself with zero clients. (Insert the sound of crickets chirping here.) I started feeling a little anxiety around this so-called dream job I had created for myself, and wondered if I had made a big mistake.

At the time, I was working with an executive coach, Jay Pryor, who taught me the principle that if you create space for something, the universe will help you fill it. I simply needed to create space, he told me. I felt like I had nothing but space, so I needed a bit of clarification. Jay explained that I needed to get more literal with it. So, I literally created space for clients by drawing ten big empty lines, spaces that I would hopefully fill with names of potential clients, on the chalkboard wall I had painted in my home office. It was truly terrifying to stare at those blanks and face the fact that I had zero clients. I was also instructed to create a mantra to manifest not just any clients, but the kind of clients that would make my job, well, a dream. I drew a magnet with a Cupid's arrow through it to represent this mantra: "I am attracting dream customers with cash." I also included space for "unexpected extras" so that I wasn't constrained by my own self-limiting goals.

A week later all ten spots on the chalkboard were filled. A week after that the unexpected extra spaces were filled with fun projects, too. This might sound a little like the Law of Attraction at work, New Age woo-woo to you, and while I personally believe there was some

universal magic at play, what the Chalkboard Method® really did was organize and guide my conscious mind into action. Tracking my progress and filling in those empty spaces was a huge confidence booster and motivated me to keep doing the work to reach my goals.

The Chalkboard Method will hold you accountable for setting big goals and seeing them through. You're literally making space for what you want.

To this day, years after my first experiment with manifesting clients, I still use the chalkboard to track and attract dream customers, grow my following, and make space for new projects, collaborations, and passive income. Every quarter it feels just as scary as the first time to create all those blank spaces waiting to be filled. Oh, and I still have my good-luck Cupid magnet and continue to create space for those unexpected extras. In fact, before we signed with an agent to write this very book, I had drawn a little book in the corner of my chalkboard! I recommend this method to each and every one of my clients as well as our podcast listeners. Like us, they're a little doubtful and resistant at first, but we always get excited emails telling us that the Chalkboard Method actually works.

The Chalkboard Method is a big visual reminder that you need to put in the work to make things happen.

THIS GOAL-SETTING SYSTEM:

• **Helps you break down long-term dreams into short-term goals.** It lays out objectives that are realistic and achievable (goodbye, overwhelming paralysis).

• **Holds you accountable for getting started and doing the work.** We all know that getting started is the hardest part. Staring at those blank spaces will light your fire.

• **Is "in your face" and easy to track.** This system doesn't replace your online systems and processes, but it does make your intentions clear and visible in your physical space so that you stay on target.

• **Uses a little bit of magic to attract the things you want.** Only if you're into that sort of thing.

But it's not enough to understand the concept. You have to actually do it.

Every time I share the Chalkboard Method with a creative entrepreneur or small business owner, I encounter skepticism. I get questions like this: "Okay, but how do I actually fill the spaces?" I get it. They want the tactics and actions that will get them the clients, but I always recommend by starting with the chalkboard. It's not enough to just understand the concept. You have to actually do it.

I recommend redoing your chalkboard quarterly. Take a photo of the past quarter's list or transfer that information to a document you can refer to later. After a year of tracking your success metrics, you can confidently begin to make predictions, see patterns, and set goals.

It's also important to mention here that I don't always fill all the spaces I create for the goals I want to hit. I've come to rely on the magic of the chalkboard so much that I trust it happens for a reason. Maybe that lack of client work is giving me an opportunity to take a vacation or rest a little. On a more practical level, not filling space on my chalkboard gives me a kick in the pants to look at what areas of my business could use improvement: I will revisit my branding, the content I'm sharing to generate leads, the work I'm putting into growing my list, and the effort

I'm putting into selling my work. You see, empty spots on my chalkboard point out where there are gaps in my plan. It allows me to see exactly where I need to change course when it comes to meeting my goals.

Emily here. When Kathleen first told me about the Chalkboard Method, I was smitten but also hesitant to replace my metric tracking systems (like client spreadsheets and accounting software) with something as "out there" and low-tech as a chalkboard and some mantras. That is until I realized that this handy tool doesn't replace them but works in partnership with how you currently track your business and personal goals. I like to think of the chalkboard as a place to get clear on what you want (in a really in-your-face way), while your usual tracking tools record what you get. The whole process has helped me turn a goal-setting habit into a full make-shit-happen routine.

HOW IT WORKS

The Chalkboard Method is a visual goal-setting system that literally makes space for what you want—whether that's new clients, more followers, or accountability to finally finish that book or digital program you've been writing. You're simply making goals and making space for them on your chalkboard, poster-board, or dry-erase board. Listen to *Being Boss,* episode 79, if you want to hear the backstory and details.

You have to actually make your chalkboard. The number one question I get from creative entrepreneurs who hear about how the Chalkboard Method has worked for me and my friends is this: "Okay, I get it. Make space. But once I do that, how do I actually fill it?" I always ask, "Have you actually made the chalkboard yet?" Please do not discredit the physical act of making the chalkboard.

A NOTE ON CLIENTS: My very first chalkboard was just ten blank spots for ten clients. If you don't do client work, your chalkboard might track paintings sold, wholesalers/retailers carrying your products, etc. Tailor it to it work for you!

UNEXPECTED EXTRAS: My executive coach Jay Pryor (listen to Episode 48 for more from him) taught me the concept of the Chalkboard Method. He instructed me to leave space for "unexpected extras," and I love the idea of making space for dreamy opportunities I haven't even imagined! This space has been filled with extra clients when I've overfilled my roster, and even amazing press like my podcast being featured on Forbes.com.

MANTRA/AFFIRMATION: Every chalkboard I've had always includes a mantra or affirmation to remind me that my success is not just about filling the blanks but about how I want to feel. One of my very first chalkboard affirmations was "I am attracting dream clients with cash." But your mantra could just be one word, like "growth" or "abundance."

There is no wrong way to do the Chalkboard Method, and you don't even need a chalkboard for it to work. For example, you could make space by pinning notecards to a corkboard or using dry-erase markers on a window. As long as you are making space for your goals in a way that is visible, the Chalkboard Method will work for you. One of the most simple yet innovative Chalkboard Method applications we've seen came from a creative entrepreneur who wanted to sell 100 spots to her online course. She outlined 100 polka dots in paint on a canvas. For each course she sold, she would fill in a polka dot with paint. Not only was she visualizing her goal, but she was making a fun piece of art on her office wall! A jewelry maker we know tacked her jewelry prototypes—bracelets, necklaces, and sets of earrings—to a wall with an empty notecard above each piece. As she sold her jewelry, she filled in the customer's name on the blank notecard above each piece. We also know a graphic designer working at a creative studio whose chalkboard includes space for one nationally recognized ad campaign and five gold medals from her annual industry awards competition. She even made space for a raise or a special bonus! These examples show how you can have fun with making space for your goals.

It's not enough to just understand the concept. You have to actually do it.

THE CHALKBOARD METHOD®

WHAT YOU'LL NEED

- A chalkboard, poster-board, dry-erase board (the idea is that it is BIG)
- Chalk or markers
- TIME: 30 minutes to 1 hour

I will be referring to whatever materials you choose to track your goals as the "chalkboard." My chalkboard was literally a wall in my office painted with chalkboard paint—so get creative and make it your own!

1. WHAT DO YOU WANT TO TRACK?

Here are a few things I've tracked over the years:
- New clients
- Speaking gigs
- Side/passion projects
- Social media followers
- Newsletter list
- Unexpected extras

2. ESTABLISH A TIMELINE

I recommend tracking your chalkboard on a quarterly timeline, but you could do monthly or yearly. I like breaking my year into quarters because it gives me just enough time to commit to my goals without getting overwhelmed by them. Quarterly, though, is short enough that you can take action daily to make your goals into a dream come true.

Here's what a typical chalkboard might look like for Braid Creative:

BRAID CREATIVE Q1 2016 — WE KNOW OUR CLARITY
OF PURPOSE: WE HELP GIVE
CREATIVES CONFIDENCE.

Braid Method Clients
JANUARY: FEBRUARY: MARCH: BRAID METHOD ECOURSE:
_____   _____   _____   JAN_____   FEB_____   MAR_____

_____   _____   _____   UNEXPECTED EXTRA

_____   _____   _____   _____   _____

Speaking And Travel (All Of 2016):   NEW PROJECTS
_____   _____   The Being Boss Podcast
_____   _____   Newsletter List-Building Campaign

NOW IT'S YOUR TURN!

I always begin by making a list on paper of the projects and goals I have. Then I'll sketch out my layout before I take it to the actual chalkboard.

LIST YOUR GOALS AND WHAT YOU WANT:

_____   _____

_____   _____

_____   _____

WRITE YOUR MANTRA, AFFIRMATION, OR EVEN QUARTERLY THEME:

_____

USE THIS SPACE TO SKETCH YOUR CHALKBOARD LAYOUT.

(Don't forget to make it real in your space—that's where the magic happens!)

Money-making habits:

HOW AND WHAT YOU SELL OR OFFER:
You'd be surprised at how many people don't clearly articulate how you can buy their services, offerings, or products, both in person and online.

INVOICING:
You can't get paid until you invoice your customers.

TRACKING EXPENSES:
Do not save adding up receipts and expenses for the end of the year. Get into the habit of tracking and automating your expenses on a daily or weekly basis.

BUDGETING:
It is as simple as seeing what's coming in (that's your income) and what's going out (your expenses). This is simple math, people! Budgeting is not a once-and-done kind of thing—it's an ongoing practice that keeps you in control of your money.

TALKING ABOUT MONEY:
Money conversations can be seen as taboo, awkward, or even crass, but getting in the habit of talking about money without weirdness can help you make more of it.

Once your goals are set, it's up to you to beeline your way to success, and setting priorities is the habit that will get you there the fastest. Goals are achieved one step at a time; priorities help you identify which step you take next.

Where focus goes, energy flows.

—TONY ROBBINS

As you become more boss, you're going to have a lot of opportunities, tasks, and decisions to make. Knowing how to prioritize what action or choice will make the most impact right now is a skillset you need to hone.

Here are a few questions we make a habit of asking ourselves to determine our priorities:
- Is this the best use of my time?
- What's most important right now?
- Is this aligned with my values?
- Could I delegate this?
- What do I want to be known for?
- How do I want to be spending my time all day?
- What is my deadline? What needs to happen next?

NON-NEGOTIABLES

"Non-negotiables" help you create steadfast boundaries, habits, and routines for the things in your life that are of the utmost priority. Non-negotiables often make everything else in your life run smoothly—if your non-negotiable is neglected or broken, nothing else seems to work quite right.

For us, non-negotiable items include:
- A daily walk or workout
- Getting at least eight hours of sleep
- Being present for our kiddos' big moments
- Publishing quality content every single week
- What are yours?

SETTING INTENTIONS

You already have intentions, whether or not you realize it. As you read this book, you're intending to learn some things that can help you be more boss. When you're done, you may pick up your phone with the intention of making reservations for dinner so you don't go to bed hungry. Intentions, big or small, shape your actions all day, every day, and it's up to you how mindfully or consciously you shape your reality with those intentions. If your intentions remain unconscious, you will always be a victim of your own circumstance, going along for the ride of your life rather than choosing where you go and what you create.

Your goals mean shit if you feel like shit along the way.

So, if you ask us what our favorite boss habit is, it is intention setting. Setting intentions is purposefully bringing conscious attention to how you want to move through life. For example, if you wake up one morning with a lot of errands on your schedule, you might approach the day with an intention of *efficiency*. You have a lot to do in a small amount of time, and making an effort to be efficient will keep you focused on not wasting time or energy. If you don't create a conscious intention that will support your goal of completing all your errands, you might find yourself feeling frazzled and rushed or end your day without getting it all done. So do you want to run errands like a boss or not? It's your choice. How you choose to tackle a full day is just a small example of how you can bring intentions into your daily life. Setting monthly and even yearly intentions can make a big difference in how you actively participate in shaping your reality in all aspects of your life—from your relationships and home to your business and career.

Setting intentions is a practice in mindfulness. When you're practicing intentions, you're aware of what you need at any given moment, and you're tapping into the state of being that will most help you feel the way you want to feel while helping you find success. We've adopted this practice to help us be mindful of what we desire and proactive about cultivating not only the *thing* but the *feeling* in our lives. Perhaps you have a day that calls for *focus* or a month that needs a little more *kindness*. Recognizing your needs and committing not only to practicing those intentions but also to identifying where they're already abundant in your life will set you on a path toward any goal in a way that resonates with you.

We've made a routine of setting monthly intentions that guide our actions for the month. We've used these intentions to help us find *discipline* during busy months, *grace* when we're trying new things, and to be *articulate* when our calendars are filled with speaking engagements. Here's how we do it:

1. Take a broad look at your projects and priorities for the month. Do you have a lot of client work, personal projects, or content creation? Maybe you've lined up speaking gigs, podcast recordings, or workshops. Or maybe a big family vacation.

2. Check in on how you feel about the tasks at hand and get a sense of what values or feelings you need more of during the month. Perhaps you need to dedicate your month to *organization* (great for kicking off new projects or tightening up your ship), *balance* (perfect if you're overwhelmed), or *magic* (if you want to appreciate the wonder around you).

3. Set your intention. It's usually a one-word intention or a short mantra. Write it at the top of your to-do list or on a sticky note on your laptop.

Now, it's key to set up your daily routine to remind you of the intentions you want to cultivate and to enable you to practice them. It's easy enough to set your intention, but it's up to you to find a way to remind yourself and hold yourself accountable to your intention. Schedule it into your calendar, set daily reminder alarms on your phone, or share your intention with a close friend or even your community. If you don't get it perfect every day, that's okay! Practicing your intention is about taking action repeatedly until

Some of our favorite intentions:

ORGANIZATION

As creative entrepreneurs we aren't at a loss for ideas and talent, but organizing intentionally can bring much-needed systems and processes to the *business* of doing what you love.

ARTICULATE

Sometimes it's hard to communicate all those ideas in a consistent and cohesive way—the intention to articulate helps you say things concisely.

REST

When you're hustling all day, every day, the intention to rest can balance out the threat of burnout.

ENTHUSIASM

When you're feeling weighed down by the daily grind, intending to be enthusiastic about your work can rekindle that original spark of why you chose to do the damn thing in the first place.

you get proficient at living in a way that feels totally boss on your terms.

The point is to put your intention at the forefront of your daily life so that you can work every day to recognize the good that you already have, and continue to cultivate more of it in your life. This way you can practice your values and reach your goals with meaning, and be present in the process along the way.

ONE-WORD INTENTIONS

Make intention setting very simple by choosing a single word to represent what you want to focus on. This word becomes your intention.

DAILY: Set an intention for the day to help you hone in on the task at hand. For example, your intention might be *competence* on a day when you're pitching to a potential client.

MONTHLY: You can also pick a one-word intention for the month, giving you something to practice in all aspects of your life and work during that time. Having a one-word intention allows you to experience your world through a different lens with every new theme, and makes you more mindful of taking steps toward what you want.

YEARLY: Beyond your day or your month, you can also use a one-word intention for an entire year. We like to do this practice every year for our business. If you're not a fan of making New Year's resolutions, a one-word intention is a great alternative (and conversation piece!). We've had *The Year of Growth*, *The Year of Joy*, and *The Year of Balance*, with each intention driving our decisions and actions for the entire year.

RITUALS

Rituals are routines that have been kicked up a notch, making them more meaningful to you than your daily practices of brushing your teeth or taking the dog for a walk. Whereas habits and routines are repeated so often that you can do them without thinking, rituals are devices that return your attention fully to what you're doing. These are exercises that bring you back from your long list of to-dos and big dreamy goals to ground you in *right now*.

Many creatives ritualize their morning writing, pouring their same cup of coffee, sitting in the same chair, and using the same pen to write in their journal. It's a meaningful experience that makes this part of their day sacred. It gets them in the right mindset to tackle their day on a deeper, even more visceral, level, just as athletes ritualize their pre-game routines. Many business owners ritualize monthly goal setting or that thing they do at the end of each business day to shut it off and walk away. You can ritualize any part of your process as a way to give it more energy and focus, and therefore make it more impactful for the outcome you desire. It's a process that you know gets you into your winning mindset. You give it the attention it deserves, as it plays a big part in your success. You practice rituals because you believe they hold a bit of—dare we say—*magic*.

Choose your rituals wisely and practice them faithfully, because they energize your body and your mind and will positively affect your ongoing performance.

INTENTION-SETTING RITUALS

We just discussed creating intentions to guide your actions and explained how you can use a one-word intention to help you work and live mindfully based on how you want to feel. We know that this is effective for helping us reach our goals—we've done it for years and the practice connects us to and engages us with our own lives, so it's an ongoing part of our greater success-focused routine. This practice is a constant reminder that we hold our present and our future in our hands, that we're the bosses of our own lives, and we can live and work however we want. We share our intentions with those closest to us as a way to hold ourselves accountable to focusing on and cultivating what we want from our actions. When we speak our intentions out loud, it brings them into the real world.

In fact, it's so important to us that it's not just another regular, by-the-calendar, monthly routine. It's an intention-setting ritual we do based on the cycles of the moon. For years we set intentions based on the calendar months, but as creatives with our faces constantly in our computer screen, we found ourselves craving more practices that take place in the "real world," so we ditched our calendars, moved away from the screen, and went outside to look up at the moon. And because the moon works in a twenty-seven- to twenty-eight-day cycle, we have enough time to fully practice our intentions and get to squeeze thirteen intentions out of a calendar year, instead of just twelve. Here's is what this ritual looks like:

On each new moon, light a candle, get out your journal, and answer these questions:

• **What things am I grateful for?** (The answer to this is often a simple list.)

• **What was my intention for the previous month?** How did it show up in my life? How did it challenge me?

• **Explore your intention for the upcoming month.** If a new intention for the upcoming cycle hasn't been chosen yet, spend a few moments free-writing about whatever comes to mind, whether it's a struggle, a current situation or opportunity, or something you're interested in. In particular, write about your desired outcome. Be mindful of the feelings that come up when writing out the outcome, or any feeling-words you write down (especially if they get written down over and over). Choose an intention that fits this writing.

• **What is my intention for the next month?** How is this feeling already present in my life? How do I plan to practice more of this new intention? How do I imagine it will present itself?

• **What goals do I wish to accomplish in this next cycle?**

When you're done, blow out your candle and walk away. Ritual done. Path set. Ready to go.

The moon represents our feeling world, our emotional world, our subconscious.

—EZZIE SPENCER, *BEING BOSS*, EPISODE 74

When we decided to include the idea of setting intentions with the moon in our book, we thought it might be a little too woo-woo—but here's the deal: the moon is a natural time tracker that gets us away from our screens and back into nature. The moon has not only a physical effect on the gravitational pull we experience on Earth (just look at the ocean tides) but also a cultural significance that we think is worth recognizing. We pulled in our friend Ezzie Spencer to share how setting intentions with the phases of the moon can make you a little more boss.

EZZIE SPENCER: In many different cultures over time, the moon has been associated with themes such as fertility, abundance, and agriculture. Taking up this symbolism, at each new moon, I plant a fresh seed—an intention for what I would like to cultivate in my life in the month ahead.

At the next new moon, you may wish to invite something material into your life. For example, you may wish to set an intention for your business to flourish with new clients and accompanying financial abundance. Or, your new moon intention could be more intangible: to cultivate more stability, peace, ease, flow, trust, joy, patience, or compassion.

The new moon is just the first of the eight phases in the moon cycle. Rather than set an intention at this first phase and then neglect it, you will optimize your chances of success with your intention by nourishing it throughout the entire moon cycle, which lasts about a month.

You can do this by returning to your intention each day in the cycle: journal about your experience, and anchor your intention by feeling it in your body. The more you pay attention to your desires, and take effective action based on this, the more likely you are to make your dreams real.

In the Lunar Abundance practice, the moon cycle is divided into eight phases, with each phase lasting for three or four days. These eight phases come in pairs, classified as yang (doing) and yin (being) phases. I've found that we need both "doing" and "being" to be effective *and* take good care of ourselves.

Rather than always hustling and pushing forward, it is essential to our well-being to slow down, at times, to reflect and restore. Pausing also helps us to see the path forward more clearly, and can help us see a solution when we are refreshed. For example, rather than getting lost in a spiral of worry about a lack of clients in a yin phase, we might take a walk or a bath or an early night and, when refreshed, see we have missed an obvious step that we could take, such as reaching out to a potential lead or starting a specific new promotional activity.

The reality is that life and work will never be fully yang or fully yin, but these alternating phases offer permission for both rest and action. I work with the moon cycle as a tool for reflection and a natural timekeeper. You can pop the moon phases into your calendar, stay connected with your intention, and take the time to develop the most effective action.

If we allow her, the moon may inspire our dreams, beckon us to create the life that we secretly feel we want to lead, and nudge us toward taking the most discerning action to make our intentions materialize—in a gentle, effective, and sustainable way.

Dr. Ezzie Spencer is the host of an iTunes podcast and the author of a book on how to work with the moon cycles to cultivate joy, peace, and purpose. Her concept, Lunar Abundance®, marries intellect with intuition and has reaped results for many women through one-on-one coaching sessions and the support of a flourishing online community at www.lunarabundance.com and @lunarabundance on Instagram.

Journaling: the habit, routine, and ritual

Making time to write down a part of our daily routine is one of our favorite ways to stay in tune with our intentions and to process emotions, questions, desires, and more to move along from dreaming and scheming to taking action. A journaling or writing practice is often the key that unlocks a wealth of power for creatives. By privately expressing your thoughts and emotions, you're able to process them and come out on the other side to find a clear path. It sets you up for taking action toward your goal with your intentions in hand—an important habit for any creative entrepreneur.

PROMPTS FOR JOURNALING:

- WHAT IS MY BIGGEST CHALLENGE RIGHT NOW? HOW CAN I TURN IT INTO AN OPPORTUNITY?

- WHAT IS MY GREATEST DESIRE? WHAT ACTIONS OR BEHAVIORS WILL HELP ME FEEL THE WAY I WANT TO FEEL?

- WHAT AM I WORKING ON TODAY? WHERE DO I NEED HELP?

- I'M GRATEFUL FOR . . .

- WRITE A LETTER TO YOUR PAST SELF THAT TELLS YOU WHAT TO LOOK FORWARD TO AND WHAT NOT TO WORRY ABOUT.

Habits and routines are how you implement a boss mindset and solid boundaries.

- DOES YOUR DAY HAVE THE STRUCTURE YOU CRAVE?
  IF NOT, WHAT DOES YOUR DREAM DAY LOOK LIKE?

- ARE YOU TAKING CARE OF YOUR BODY IN A WAY THAT FUELS YOUR WORK?

- WHAT KIND OF GOALS DO YOU WANT TO MAKE SPACE
  FOR WITH THE CHALKBOARD METHOD®?

- HOW DO YOU WANT TO FEEL AS YOU WORK
  TO ACHIEVE YOUR GOALS?

CHAPTER 5:

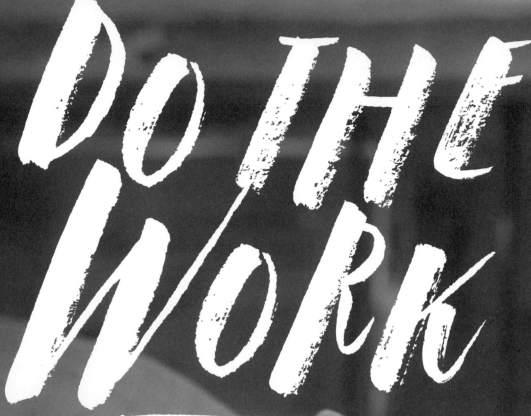

DO THE WORK

Do the work.
Get paid.
Make it rain.

It is possible for you to make money doing things that you love doing. We do it. We've talked to bosses in numerous fields who are doing it. And we absolutely believe that you can too. That's why we've written this whole book: this is us giving you permission to make money—*good* money!—and do work that you enjoy doing, because you don't have to hate your job. You don't have to marry yourself to a corporation in order to feel secure, make a steady paycheck, and someday retire. And you sure as hell don't have to do the same old thing for the rest of your life.

But you better bet that making money doing what you love is a little more complicated than reprogramming your boundaries and setting up fresh habits for yourself. You actually have to *make money* doing the thing you love, and that's where being an entrepreneur comes into play.

In this chapter, we're breaking down some mindsets, boundaries, habits, and exercises that apply directly to how you sell your expertise and make money doing it. We'll get you thinking like an entrepreneur about how you make money, brand yourself as an expert, and make moves in your business to help you build a career doing the work that you want to be known for. A boss knows how to do the work, and get paid.

THE SIMPLE BUSINESS PLAN

If you don't know what goes into a formal business plan, fret not. You can start and run a super-legit business without one, and you don't need a degree or a fancy consultant to help you figure it out. Here's what you need to know to topline your business vision:

• **Write down how much money you want to net this year.** "Net" means the money you make after expenses and taxes.

• **List your streams of revenue.** This list includes all the different services, products, and offerings you sell to make money.

• **Write down your job title and make a list of your duties.** This is the first step to creating your own personal organizational chart.

• **List where in your business you need help.** This can include the little things you don't like to do or big things you need expert help with.

• **Write down your mission.** You need to know what purpose your business serves to filter and process all the decisions you have to make along the way, but this doesn't have to be formal.

• **Write down a list of how you want to feel along the way.** Focusing on how you want to feel in the process of building and growing a business is what separates the fulfilled creative entrepreneurs from the miserable ones.

BE A FARMER

Farmers wake up early and do the work. They get their hands dirty and plant seeds. They protect and nurture their land for months and years before they're able to harvest their crops. They look at the big picture and they practice patience. Anytime you begin to feel anxiety or worry over your business, get to farming. (Okay, I'm not literally telling you to buy some land and get some goats—that's a fantasy for another day.) Wake up early, do the work, build your brand, be a student of your craft, nurture relationships, and share your expertise along the way . . . that's farming. If you want to grow your business, your brand, and your bottom line, first you have to plant the seeds.

BE A HUNTER

Hunting is what most people think of when they think about "hustling" for their business. Most creatives feel more comfortable as "farmers," but if you find yourself hungry it's a good idea to know how to hunt. Hunting looks like hitting the pavement and asking for work: making phone calls, sending emails, and explicitly telling people how to hire you. The trick with hunting is not going after the kill with desperation but with the confidence and ease of a jaguar that knows what it wants.

THE HOT SHIT LIST

You know what a shit list is, right? It's that list of people who have wronged, disrespected, or simply annoyed you. It's the people who are energy drains and feel toxic to be around. For the creative entrepreneur it can be the client from hell or a pesky copycat. We personally don't have a shit list here at *Being Boss*. We don't like to focus our energy on what we don't like or want in our lives. But we *do* have a "hot shit" list. This is a list of people we admire, respect, and would love to be around more—and we use this list to cultivate relationships and clients. Here's how it works:

- **Make a list of 200 people (yes, 200—we know it's a lot, but that's the point).** Your list can be on paper or in a spreadsheet.
- **Your list can include anybody from an acquaintance you silently admire to someone like Oprah.** Nobody is too big or small to make it onto the list.
- **Include emails, URLs, and social media handles next to names for reference.**
- **Begin following, subscribing to newsletters, hiring, or interacting with the names on your list.** You'd be surprised how many genuine connections you can make by simply showing up.

PERSONAL BRANDING

Sometimes creative entrepreneurs act as if they have to ditch their personality to be seen as "professional" once they start working for themselves. The reality is that people work with people, and who you are is an asset to your business. It's not enough to have a service or product to sell—you have to communicate what it is you do and make a memorable first impression on your potential dream client. That's branding, and it's a huge part of how you will make money doing what you love.

When you think about branding, the first things that may come to mind are a logo, a color scheme, typography standards, slogans, and taglines. And while a visual identity is an important piece of the puzzle, a brand is so much more than just a logo. A brand sets the tone, intention, and boundaries for what you choose to write, share, show, and say about your business. Your brand lives in your personal style, in your space online and offline, in conversations and emails, and on social media.

Your personal brand helps you create an expectation, and even make a promise, of what you're all about. It helps define who you are before you ever begin explaining what you do. As creatives, explaining our work and why we do it isn't always traditional or clear-cut, which can leave us uncertain, apologetic, and even tongue tied. This kind of stumbling over words risks leaving our potential customers confused and can make us sound unemployed rather than self-employed.

Beyond coming across like the professional you are, you have to remember that business is personal. *People buy from people*, and the more you can blend who you are, your personality, your values, your stories, and your interests into your professional brand, the more creatively fulfilled and aligned you will feel in your work—from the customers you attract to the projects you pursue.

YOUR BRAND IS THE OUTER LAYER

The tricky thing about branding yourself is that you know, and we know, that there is so much more to you than that first impression. You've got passion! And talent! And all the smarts! And you're going to want to share all those things in an instant. But the point of branding is that it's the outer layer that lets people (i.e., peers, bosses, dream customers and followers, and not-so-dreamy customers and followers) know what you're about and what they can expect to learn from you if they care to venture past the surface. An outer layer, unlike what the name implies, isn't just about how you look or what you wear, though that certainly plays a part. We're creatives, and many of us are visual creatives, so our own exterior styling can be an expression of our brand. But our outer layer can also be how we tell stories, how we're intuitive or empathic, how we are great listeners, or how we always cut to the chase.

The outer layer not only makes an impression but also hints at the deeper content and conversations that unfold along with the layers of you and your business. You can think of content as writing, sharing, or explaining what you do, but also think of content as conversations: the working, learning, networking, selling, and sharing conversations that are constantly defining and redefining those boundaries of who you are—and what you do.

BUT WHAT IF I DON'T WANT A PERSONAL BRAND?

Ooh, I feel you. Emily here—I used to say the same thing. But even as I've built a number of "not-personal" brands and spent years helping clients decide if they want to brand their business as their name or as something far less personal, I've learned an important lesson: all brands are personal. Even if you have no desire to use your name as your business name, or even have your face on your About page, you will still use your values—even if nothing else—to brand, run, and grow your business. And what is more personal than that?

WHAT DO YOU WANT TO BE KNOWN FOR?

The beautiful thing about on-point branding is that it closes the gap between how others perceive you and how you talk—and even think—about yourself. The more accurately you are able to position yourself as an expert and then deliver on that expertise, the more people are going to trust and buy you. On the flip side, the better you are at instantly articulating who you are and what you want to be known for, from the moment someone visits your website or has a conversation with you, the more you are going to repel those who aren't a good fit before they can get any further. Good branding becomes the gatekeeper that attracts the kinds of customers, projects, and opportunities you actually want with a big neon "WELCOME!" sign, and repels the ones you don't want with a big "NO, THANK YOU" sign.

CREATING COMPELLING CONTENT

We know there's more to who you are and the work you do than just the "packaged" outer layer of your brand. That's where creating content comes in. The content you develop helps you go deeper with your expertise, explore new ideas, and attract those just-right dream customers.

Consistently creating content is one of the best ways you can "farm" your business. The seeds you plant today will come to harvest months or even years from now. So even if you feel that nobody is picking up what you're putting down, the crops you nurture today will attract the dream customers you want tomorrow.

Types of content:
• Blogs
• Newsletters
• Books
• Worksheets
• Public speeches
• Podcasts
• Videos
• Social media

BUT WHAT DO I WRITE, TALK ABOUT, OR SHARE?

Can't think of what kind of content to create? The best advice we can give is to just start creating. It doesn't have to be perfect, and being boss is about hitting publish before it's perfect.

Here are a few prompts to get you started:
• What are the questions you already get?
• What kind of advice do your friends come to you for?
• What is the number one thing your audience craves?
• What is the biggest problem your audience experiences?
• What kind of conversations are you already having?

Remember! Your content shouldn't be a thinly veiled sales pitch. You want to keep it both generous and genuine. Trust that your followers will pay you more when you establish yourself as an expert they can grow to trust.

Creating content will not only help you find your voice and deepen your expertise—it will also allow you to explore new ideas and carve out a niche.

For example, let's say you're a graphic designer who is obsessed with health and nutrition. You can begin writing more about yoga, clean eating, and green smoothies while using your design skills to make your content visually stunning. From there you may begin to attract a following of yogis and foodies. Who do you think they're going to call when they need a designer to brand their new studio or design their next cookbook? Another example might be a candlemaker who is inspired by her world travels. Her candles are made with fragrances that remind her of a temple in Nepal or a beach in Tulum—she's openly sharing her travels and lifestyle with her fans, whether or not they buy a candle. The story behind the product makes the purchase that much more meaningful.

What you write and the content you create shapes, in many ways, what you become.

—TARA STREET, *BEING BOSS*, EPISODE 56

GIVE IT ALL AWAY

Kathleen here. When I first started blogging in 2008, I was mostly sharing personal stuff. I was writing about decorating my historic home, describing the vacations I was taking, posting photos daily of my outfits, and sharing my culinary adventures of eating as locally as possible. Then in 2010, when I decided to leave my day job as a senior art director in advertising to be my own boss, I naturally started blogging about the new journey of working for myself. Blogging about freelancing and entrepreneurship was a way to process the experience, find confidence in the face of uncertainty, and document what was working and what wasn't. Soon I began getting questions from other working creatives who were seeking advice about everything from client management to work-life balance to time management. Even though I felt unqualified to give any sort of business advice, since I was new to this myself, I started publicly sharing my answers to those questions on my blog.

By so openly and transparently writing about working for myself, I unintentionally positioned myself as a trustworthy expert on the subject of being my own boss. I remember thinking, "If I share all my secrets, won't I be teaching my competition how to do what I do? If I give away my knowledge for free, who will ever want to hire me?" But the funny thing is, the more I shared, the more I got hired. I was able to raise my rates and make more money than ever before.

When I started a branding company with my sister, most agencies weren't openly sharing their knowledge or their "secret sauce," but through experience I became confident that giving away everything we knew about branding in our content was the best way to position ourselves as experts right out of the gate. We were profitable and comfortable in our first year of business, and I credit the generous content we were sharing for that immediate success.

FINDING YOUR VOICE

The number one question we get from creative entrepreneurs who are wanting to blend more of who they are into the content they create is "How do I find my voice?" You find your voice by using it. Trust us, everyone struggles with showing up—we all cringe at our early work. Reading some of our early blog posts reminds us of reading our diaries from middle school! Perfectionism and our own ego can tell us we're not ready—that it's not good enough. But you won't become the writer and speaker you want to be without hitting publish and literally using your voice. It takes consistent practice to really get into the groove of articulating what you have to say and being who you are 100 percent of the time in the content you share. Here are a few tricks for getting started and keeping it real:

• **"What I really want to tell you is . . . "** Anytime you're feeling vague or unmotivated, simply open a blank document and write down, "What I really want to tell you is . . ." Start hammering away at the keyboard and don't overthink it.

 • **Create content for just one person.** Pretend as if the blog post you're writing is actually a letter to just ONE client, follower, or friend. Think about that one person and his specific problem. Write as if you're directly writing to him. You'd be surprised how getting specific for just one person will resonate with hundreds.

 • **Would I say this out loud?** It's easy to become disconnected from your content by trying to sound like the "professional" expert you want to be seen as. So try reading your content out loud and see how the words sound coming out of your mouth. You might find that your sentences are too long or that you're using jargon or words you don't usually say.

 • **How could I be more honest?** The more you can pull from real experience, examples, and personal stories, the more honest your content will be—and truth always resonates the most.

CONSISTENCY BREEDS LEGITIMACY

Your brand gives you guidelines for how you share your business with the world and how you deliver what you sell to those who buy you. Your brand defines your color scheme, fonts, voice, and mission, but it also defines how you interact with customers and market your services. A consistent brand is what makes you look like a professional—even if you're a professional with a half sleeve and a mohawk.

Reliably showing up and following these guidelines every damn time is the key to reassuring potential customers that you're the most trustworthy pro in the pack. Because consistency breeds legitimacy. When someone hears you repeatedly using the same language to talk about what you do, they begin to trust what you're saying. Consistently following your brand standards—using the same color schemes, fonts, and photo filters—will clue people into your ability to deliver like a pro. If you have an email newsletter landing in your customer's inbox every Thursday morning at 9 a.m., they begin to anticipate you being there. With consistency you build trust—and when your customer trusts you, it's easier for them to give you money.

Consistency isn't just about branding, either—it branches out to all aspects of your business. Your business should have cohesive profiles on everything from your website to your social media platforms. You use the same voice in blog posts and social media that you use in conversations and customer service emails. Treat your potential customers the same way that you treat your paying customers. Publish your blog posts, newsletters, and podcasts consistently. It doesn't have to be daily, but it should be on a regular schedule. Bringing consistency to your systems and processes—from scheduling planning meetings to checking in with your money—will make you feel more legit in your business.

> ## A business model is a system for creating, delivering, and exchanging value.
>
> —TARA GENTILE,
> *BEING BOSS*, EPISODE 92

If the business side of being a creative entrepreneur makes you feel out of your depth, you're not alone. Most of us didn't study business in school, but that shouldn't hold anyone back from making money (and good money!) doing what they love for a living. Our very own business mentor, Tara Gentile, is a genius at making business approachable and getting all of us a little more excited about it.

BEING BOSS: The phrase "business model" can sound fancy or intimidating to a new entrepreneur. How do you define it?

TARA GENTILE: Your business model is simply the system you use to create, deliver, and exchange value. Or, in more straightforward terms, your business model is the system you use to get paid for creating something people really want.

BB: So for example, if you are a website developer, clients give you money to deliver a well-designed and functional website to them. The system that gets your potential customer from knowing what you do (develop websites), to hiring and paying you (to develop their website), to the final delivery (of the website) is your business model. "Value" is a word that doesn't seem entirely tangible. What does it mean to create value for your customer?

TG: "Creating value" means creating a change for your customers: helping them do something faster, with less hassle, or with less anxiety. Whether you sell a physical product, a digital product, or a service, your customers want to accomplish something. What you offer is just a tool to help them achieve that. When they do achieve it, you've created value for them.

The way you "deliver value," then, is through that tool—your product or service. This tends to be where business owners get hung up. They put all their focus on the delivery mechanism and forget about what they're actually delivering.

Finally, you can't get paid if you don't include a way to "exchange value" with your customer. Getting paid tends to bring up a lot of demons for a new entrepreneur—but it doesn't have to.

First, remember that money—currency—is just one form of value. You create another form of value—the change the customer wants—and you ask for money in return. As long as the two sides of the exchange balance, everyone is happy.

The bottom line, when considering your business model, is to remember that it's a system. You don't want just a mishmash of products or services. You need to have a set of offers (generally not more than two to three) that work together and encourage customers to grow with your business.

BB: What do you want every creative entrepreneur to know about business models?

TG: Your business model is also a plan for the relationship that you want your customers to have with your business over time. Ideally, customers will stick around and buy multiple products or services from you because the value you create for them helps them achieve more than they could on their own.

To continue with the example of the web designer, after you complete your customer's website, you may continue to sell them ongoing site maintenance on retainer, or have a strategy for checking in on site updates or redesigns every six to twelve months.

Remember that more offers doesn't equal more money. Just like in any dating relationship, you don't want things to get complicated. Make your business model simple and straightforward. Focus on having just one to three core offers that work together to help your customer become who they want to become and help them become an evangelist for your brand.

BB: How can defining your business model help you make more money or achieve more success?

TG: The biggest benefit of better defining your business model is that it saves you time (and hassle . . . and headaches, although, I suppose that's more than one benefit). Most business owners create, create, create and then forget to actually market what they've created. They think the only way to make more money is to make something new.

A web designer without a clear business model won't have a process they've mastered or an offering they can easily market or opportunities for upselling their clients for years to come. Instead, they'll find themselves always scraping by project-to-project and earning about the same thing every year—no matter how hard they work.

The real money is in going deep with each thing you create. Everytime you create a sales campaign for a product you already have on the "shelf," you don't have to work as hard to sell it as before. You already have systems in place, and people are already familiar with the product.

Plus, when you have a clearly defined business model, your products help to sell each other. For every hour of work you put into selling one offer, you're saving time on selling others because of the natural systems behind your business. Once your customers have a taste of what you do, they're going to want more, and your business model ensures that you make that easy for them.

Tara Gentile is the founder of CoCommercial, a digital small-business community for entrepreneurs serious about making money, impacting their communities, and transforming the lives of those they love. She's also the host of Profit. Power. Pursuit., *a podcast that takes you behind the scenes of successful small businesses. Learn more at www.taragentile .com.*

What's working, what's kinda working, what's not working

Every so often (as in every quarter or two, or when we're feeling the financial heat or desire to level up), we like to sit down with one of our favorite list-making exercises to review how we're making money.

Here's how you do it:

1. Take a piece of paper and make three columns. Label them "What's Working," "What's Kinda Working," and "What's Not Working."

2. Under "What's Working," write down all the things that you're focusing on, that bring in money, or both—that you feel good about.

3. Under "What's Kinda Working," write down everything that you feel "eh" about. Maybe these things earn money but take too much management. Or maybe you feel really good about them, but they're not bringing in enough money yet.

4. Under "What's Not Working," write down everything that's not working, the things that are not paying you back for the energy you put into them.

5. Now look at your list and take stock:

• What would happen if you were to remove what's not working?

• What actions do you need to take to move items from "What's Kinda Working" to "What's Working"?

• What could you accomplish if you spend all your extra energy only on the things that are already working?

• What if you were to do something really crazy and remove everything except for the one or two things that are working the best, and double your efforts there?

This exercise always clarifies the types of work that drain you and the ones you should focus more energy on, and these questions will initiate some "what if" questioning that will have you thinking outside the box in terms of where and how you focus your energy in your work. It's all about focusing on what's getting results, taking the necessary action to make sure anything that could work is fulfilling its potential, and shedding light on things that could free up energy if you were to simply let them go.

For example, let's say you make money doing graphic design, with affiliate partnerships, and through a little bit of business coaching and consulting on the side. Alongside those offerings you are marketing what you do and positioning yourself as an expert by writing blog posts, recording podcasts, and sharing your work on social media. The more stuff on your plate, the more important it is to do this exercise so you can see where your efforts are working . . .

or not. You can see here how this creative would do this exercise:

WHAT'S WORKING:

- Graphic design clients who want strategic branding: *it's working because it pays you well, and you feel like an expert.*
- Sharing your work on social media: *it acts as an in-the-moment portfolio that attracts dream customers who love work.*
- Recording podcasts: *it's fun and gets engagement from listeners.*

For "what's working" items, how could you better leverage or double down on these opportunities?

WHAT'S KINDA WORKING:

- Blogging: *it's only kind of working because you love writing, but you're not getting much interaction.*
- Affiliate partnerships: *it's easy, but it doesn't make a lot of money.*
- Business coaching: *there are blurred lines between the branding projects and the coaching projects that confuse the issue of how you charge your client.*

For these "kinda working" items, how could you make them work better for you? What do you need to do to move them to the "what's working" list? Or, what if you were to stop doing them altogether?

WHAT'S NOT WORKING:

- One-off invitation and project design: *it's not working because it doesn't pay you well and these clients treat you like an order-taker.*

Consider scratching these "not working" items from your to-do list. Maybe not forever, but at least for now, while you focus on building other parts of your business. If it's on your "not working" list, then this is your permission to let it go.

How do I get more customers?

Even if you are the edgiest, or friendliest, or coolest, or most relatable goofball around—you have to be confident in your own expertise and what you're selling.

—TARA STREET, BRAID CREATIVE

Anytime we need a little clarity around anything to do with branding or positioning ourselves as the creative experts we are, Tara Street is our go-to gal. She's not only the co-founder of Braid Creative, but she's also Kathleen's big sister. We've brought in Tara in case you need some big-sister guidance about getting more dream customers. (Don't we all wish we had a big sis like Tara?!)

BEING BOSS: What's a good way to know who your dream customer actually is?

TARA STREET: Think about someone you've worked with in the past who was a total dream. Now, that doesn't necessarily mean that client became your best friend, doing cartwheels of joy throughout the whole process. Think more about a consistency of dreaminess throughout the process: mutual respect, trust in your guidance, work that you loved doing, with a dash of enthusiasm that made it a rewarding experience for both of you (so maybe one cartwheel moment happened). Oh, and dream customer paid you. Gladly. Willingly. Because they knew you were worth it.

BB: What if you've never worked with a dream customer?

TS: How do you know who they are, and how do you get them to hire you? If you've never had a dreamy client experience, ask why. Is it because you've said yes to anyone willing to pay you? Is it because you just haven't had very many clients to start with? Or is it because you're not guiding the client expectations with a clear direction or structure—so you overcompensate, over-deliver, and end up regretting the engagement, resenting the client, and hating the pickle you got yourself in?

If you said "yes" to one or all of the above, the problem may not be the client, but your offering. You need a dream offering that has a beginning, middle, and end. You need a dream deliverable that's clearly defined, so you can set an expectation for your clients of what they actually get, your role, and what they will experience along the way.

But let's say you have a great offering and you're discerning about who you work with. Dare I say, you even have a niche! Terrific! But! You still don't have that dream client experience that you can point to and say, "More of them, please!"

If you haven't met them yet in person, then you're just going to have to make your dream client real in your head (or better yet, on paper) so you can start creating content that reaches out and grabs them!

What is their job? What are their pains? Stresses? Hopes? Dreams? What do they value? What do they really love? If you had to write an email directly addressed to them, what would you say? "Dear _____, let me tell you why I'm a total fit for you."

If you could bullet out a before-and-after list of what they would feel and experience working with you, what would it say? "Before you work with me you might be struggling with ___, ___, ___. After you work with me you will experience ___, ___, ___."

This is the best way to make the dream client you've never had specific, attainable, and real in your heart and mind, and create content that speaks directly to their hearts and minds in return.

BB: What's the best way to let your dream customer know you're the one for them?

TS: Here's where that confident expert part really kicks in, even if you are the edgiest, or friendliest, or coolest, or most relatable goofball around—you have to be confident in your own expertise and what you're selling. It's okay to be a little butterflies-in-the-stomach on the inside. You don't have to be a stone-cold pro. Just be yourself, but also let your guidance shine through.

For example, when you're creating sales pages on your website, writing an email or blog post to generate some client interest, replying to new client inquiries, or facilitating a great kickoff or first coffee chat, try peppering the conversation with a few of these talking points to let your dream client know you are a fit for them:

• Talk about the patterns you see in clients just like them.

• Don't fall all over yourself befriending them, flattering them, or convincing them that you're the perfect fit.

• Simply explain what you do; use past examples; keep it simple.

• Give them permission to bring up any hesitations or skepticism.

• Structure is great, but don't let an overly structured process cloud the end deliverable or result they're actually buying from you.

• Let them know you are there to create an experience customized to them, but you're not doing it from scratch—like a trail guide, you've been here before and you know the way.

Tara Street is a brand strategist, writer, and creative director and co-founder of Braid Creative & Consulting with her boss sister Kathleen Shannon. (But Tara is the oldest, so they both agree she'll always be the boss of Kathleen.) See www.braidcreative.com.

WHAT'S IN YOUR TOOLBELT?

Kathleen here. I graduated from college with a fine arts degree with one goal: to be the best graphic designer ever. Beyond the formal training I received in school, I was obsessed with studying other great designers and honing my own skills by practicing every day. Malcolm Gladwell talks about the 10,000 hours it takes to become an expert in your field, and I committed to putting in the time. But, while I loved the creativity that came with branding an NBA team and designing ads that won gold awards, I craved deeper meaning. I wanted my design skills to be used for making the world a better place, and I felt like my purpose as a creative went beyond mere graphic design. To be clear, I still absolutely use design in my business. If I'm not pushing pixels myself for my own brand, I'm using the vocabulary and language I've learned as a designer to give creative direction to my team. A shift happened in which my skills went from being my number one priority to simply becoming a tool in my toolbelt.

Emily here. I picked up my web design skills in high school, making them one of the earliest tools to find their home in my toolbelt. It never occurred to me to officially pursue web design and development in college, and no one was as surprised as me when I launched my web design business shortly after graduating. Even as I began taking my first clients, I knew I wasn't a lifelong web designer—it wasn't my path. It was simply a means to some other end that I didn't even recognize yet. Years later, I don't sell my web design services anymore. They've been tucked away in my toolbelt and removed from my business model. They served the purpose of giving me the experience of building not only websites but *businesses* in the online space, facilitating the addition of plenty of new skills to fill my toolbelt.

You too have been collecting skills and experience along the way. It's easy to feel that you should be monetizing all your skills just because you can. But remember, they are just tools in your toolbelt; your focus should be the expertise you want to be known for. Just because you can do the thing (or ALL the things) doesn't mean you need to *sell* it. It can just be there to support you along the way.

- What are the special skills and talents you have?

- What are you best at?

- What do you want to be known for?

- How do your skills support your purpose?

- What tools would you like to add to your toolbelt?

KNOW YOUR NUMBERS

Reaching goals and finding success come down to simple math. We talk about how we want to feel and what our values are, sure, but we like to use metrics so we know when we've met our goals. Numbers can be counted, which means we can track them to see if we're moving toward our goals or not.

For an easy example, let's say you value *freedom* and you decide to measure that value by the number of vacations you take each year. You set a goal of three vacations and track your progress. You know your numbers: how many you want, how many you've completed so far, and how many you have left to reach your goal. You have an easy way to track whether you're practicing your value of *freedom*.

When you're an entrepreneur, knowing your numbers takes on a whole other level of importance: How much money do you need to make? How much money have you made? How much of that money do you need to spend? Knowing these kinds of numbers not only makes you a responsible entrepreneur but gives you boundaries within which you can make decisions for your business. And these decisions will directly impact the life that you want to live.

If you're not down with numbers, find someone who can work closely with you to make sure they're being handled, or maybe get over it by starting small and practicing often. You should always be tracking your money, how you're spending your time, and whether or not you're reaching your goals. This tracking is an important part of working like a boss; making sure you know your numbers will guide you consistently toward success.

Here are some numbers you need to know:
- How many hours a week you want to work
- How many hours a week you actually work
- How much money you make
- How much money you need to survive
- How much money you need to thrive
- How much money and time it costs for you to deliver your product or service
- How many products or services you can produce in a year, given the amount of time you wish to work

SET AND TRACK MONEY GOALS FOR A YEAR

Tracking your money doesn't have to be all accounting software and spreadsheets (though those things are a necessary part of running a business and are systems you need to have in place). Sometimes the creative brain just needs a fancy piece of paper and a pen. Use this exercise to get clear about your money goals for a year, and visit it at the end of each month to track your progress along the way. This same system can be used to set and track any number-based goals you have.

MONTHLY INCOME GOALS

JANUARY

GOAL: _____

ACTUAL: _____

DIFFERENCE: +/-_____

YTD: _____

YTD DIFFERENCE:_____

FEBRUARY

GOAL: _____

ACTUAL: _____

DIFFERENCE: +/-_____

YTD: _____

YTD DIFFERENCE:_____

MARCH

GOAL: _____

ACTUAL: _____

DIFFERENCE: +/-_____

YTD: _____

YTD DIFFERENCE:_____

APRIL

GOAL: _____

ACTUAL: _____

DIFFERENCE: +/-_____

YTD: _____

YTD DIFFERENCE:_____

MAY

GOAL: _____

ACTUAL: _____

DIFFERENCE: +/-_____

YTD: _____

YTD DIFFERENCE:_____

JUNE

GOAL: _____

ACTUAL: _____

DIFFERENCE: +/-_____

YTD: _____

YTD DIFFERENCE:_____

JULY

GOAL: _____

ACTUAL: _____

DIFFERENCE: +/-_____

YTD: _____

YTD DIFFERENCE:_____

AUGUST

GOAL: _____

ACTUAL: _____

DIFFERENCE: +/-_____

YTD: _____

YTD DIFFERENCE:_____

SEPTEMBER

GOAL: _____

ACTUAL: _____

DIFFERENCE: +/-_____

YTD: _____

YTD DIFFERENCE:_____

OCTOBER

GOAL: _____

ACTUAL: _____

DIFFERENCE: +/-_____

YTD: _____

YTD DIFFERENCE:_____

NOVEMBER

GOAL: _____

ACTUAL: _____

DIFFERENCE: +/-_____

YTD: _____

YTD DIFFERENCE:_____

DECEMBER

GOAL: _____

ACTUAL: _____

DIFFERENCE: +/-_____

YTD: _____

YTD DIFFERENCE:_____

TOTAL GOAL:_____

ACTUAL: _____

TOTAL DIFFERENCE: _____

MONEY MANTRAS

What makes us entrepreneurs is our desire to turn what we love doing into profit. That said, anxiety around money is something that even the most seasoned entrepreneurs face—so we've got a few money mantras to help us be the boss of our bottom line.

Stop freaking out about money: Money woes can hijack what could otherwise be a perfectly productive day. When you're freaking out about money, you'll start reacting out of fear as opposed to being purposefully proactive. So if you're freaking out about money, take a deep breath, and STOP IT! Get back to doing what you do best—worrying will get you nowhere but deeper in your own depression.

Money is only as weird as you make it: If you're a creative who has any funny feelings of guilt or shame around talking about money—or better yet, asking to be compensated for the work you do—this mantra is for you. The more confidently you can talk about money, the more reassured your customers will feel handing it over to you. Conversations about money are only as weird as you make them (and to be a profitable creative, you're going to need to talk about money often)!

Money is energy: When you are in charge of setting your own prices, you might begin to question what money is, anyway. Money is a social construct that we've all somehow agreed to—and practically speaking, money helps us easily measure the values of goods and services we exchange with one another. When you can begin thinking of money as a flow of energy, you can ditch the money beliefs you've been holding onto and more freely collect and spend without attaching weird or negative feelings to it.

WHAT ARE SOME OF YOUR BELIEFS ABOUT MONEY? WHAT MONEY MANTRA COULD YOU ADOPT TO REWIRE YOUR MONEY BELIEFS?

WRITE YOURSELF A CHECK

First, if you're not writing yourself a regular paycheck from your business checking account, you're not treating yourself like the boss you are. Even if it's $300 a month when you're getting off the ground, it's important to get in the habit of compensating yourself for your hard work.

In 1985 comedian and movie star Jim Carrey drove to Hollywood in his beat-up Toyota. He was broke and full of big dreams. He drove up to the Hollywood Hills and parked. There, with a view overlooking the valley, he wrote himself a check for $10 million and postdated it for ten years later. Just less than a decade later he was a blockbuster star and able to cash in on his dream.

TRY THIS: WRITE YOURSELF A CHECK FOR YOUR DREAM SALARY. Literally grab a blank check from your checkbook. Write in your dream salary and postdate the check for a year or two from now. Don't sign the check yet! Keep it in a place where you'll be able to find it later when you're ready to cash in.

Don't have a checkbook? A little too 1994 for you? Just draw a check on a piece of paper.

INVEST IN YOURSELF

You've heard it a million times: you have to spend money to make money. But we're not buying it. We have bootstrapped our businesses and grown our teams with zero debt. We've paid our bills since day one and have made it a priority to invest in ourselves along the way. And trust us, there is no windfall, private investor, trust fund, or sugar daddy paying our way. The most talented and innovative entrepreneurs we know have managed to expand their capacity for success by working with what they've got and getting creative within the constraints they've been given. They're not trying to buy their way to the finish line, and neither should you. Money certainly makes some things easier, but there is no amount of cash that will guarantee success. However, you can invest in yourself along the way, in a way that doesn't break the bank and gives you little boosts of fuel that will help you level up your game.

Anytime you make a purchase in your business, it's important to ask what the return on investment is—how will the benefit justify the cost? In other words: *How will this purchase help me make more money? And how much?* By asking these questions, you can begin to figure out when to invest in your business with money and when to invest with do-it-yourself sweat equity and work with what you've got.

Technology and tools: Investing in tech and tools that help you work with more speed, quality, efficiency, and craft will enable you to create better work in less time. Now, that said, you do not need to purchase every shiny new toy that comes on the market. If you're strapped for cash, make do

Pros of partnering up:

- YOU GET TWICE THE WORK HOURS AND MORE SKILLSETS TO BRING TO THE TABLE.
- YOU HAVE SOMEONE TO BRAINSTORM WITH.
- SOMEONE IS THERE TO HOLD DOWN THE FORT WHILE YOU GO ON VACATION.
- YOU AREN'T SOLELY RESPONSIBLE FOR MAKING IT WORK.
- THEY'LL HOLD YOU ACCOUNTABLE FOR PULLING YOUR WEIGHT.
- IT'S A LITTLE LESS LONELY WHEN YOU HAVE SOMEONE IN IT WITH YOU.
- IT'S EASIER TO FOCUS ON YOUR CORE GENIUS WITH DEFINED ROLES IN PLACE.
- YOU'LL ELEVATE YOUR GAME WHEN YOU'RE MOTIVATED BY YOUR PARTNER'S STRENGTHS.
- (WE LAUGH A LOT.)

Cons of partnering up:

- WHILE SOME THINGS GET DONE FASTER WITH A PARTNER, HAVING TO BRING EVERY IDEA TO THE TABLE FOR CONSIDERATION CAN MAKE SOME THINGS MOVE A LITTLE SLOWER.
- DISAGREEMENTS CAN SUCK.
- IF ONE PERSON FEELS LIKE THEY'RE DOING MORE THAN THE OTHER, IT CAN LEAD TO HARD FEELINGS (AND HARD CONVERSATIONS).
- YOU DON'T HAVE COMPLETE CREATIVE CONTROL OVER YOUR BUSINESS.
- BUSINESS SETUP AND TAXES GET A LITTLE MORE COMPLEX.

HERE ARE IMPORTANT THINGS TO KEEP IN MIND IF YOU DECIDE TO FIND A BOSS-PARTNER:

- MAKE SURE YOU HAVE COMPLEMENTARY WORK ETHICS.
- GET A SOLID OPERATING AGREEMENT IN PLACE.
- HAVE SYSTEMS AND PROCESSES IN PLACE TO GET THINGS DONE EFFICIENTLY.
- CREATE CLEAR BOUNDARIES AROUND HOW YOU'LL BOTH WORK, SEPARATELY AND TOGETHER.
- DEFINE EACH OF YOUR ROLES (MOST OF THEM SHOULD NOT OVERLAP; YOU DON'T BOTH NEED TO BE DOING THE SAME THINGS).
- BE RESPONSIBLE FOR YOUR OWN TASKS SO YOU'RE NOT HOLDING ANYONE ELSE UP FROM DOING THEIR BEST WORK. (GET YOUR OWN SHIT DONE!)
- GET COMFORTABLE WITH HAVING HARD CONVERSATIONS.

with what you have and invest only in tools you use every single day. For example, don't buy the newest iPad with dreams of doing hand lettering on it if you're not even practicing on paper first. Don't buy a fancy new microphone for the podcast you don't yet have. Start by creating with the tools you already have until they clearly impede your progress—and THEN invest in the tools and tech that will help you take things to the next level.

Health insurance: When you work for yourself, paying for your own health care is like paying taxes. You may feel it a little harder because you don't have an employer automatically withdrawing it from your check for you, but paying for it yourself shouldn't be a deal breaker when it comes to making the decision to work for yourself. Plus, as a creative entrepreneur, you have potential to make even more than what an employer could pay you! It'll all come out in the wash.

Your office space: One of the best things about being a creative entrepreneur is the location independence that comes with the nature of our jobs. You can be a legit professional from home, a coffee shop, a beach, or your own studio space. We've tried it all, and no matter where we're working from, we've found one thing to be true: creatives need to feel at ease in their space no matter where they're working. Invest in the essentials that will inspire you while you work—whether that's a delicious-smelling candle, a standing work desk, a really comfy chair, or a bunch of plants and a co-working kitty cat.

Conferences and retreats: Most creatives don't travel enough because they decide it's a frivolous expense. But there is nothing like attending a conference or retreat to establish genuine connections that will feed your career with clients, referrals, and countless opportunities. Travel isn't an expense—it's an investment. When you travel for business, be sure to set an intention, "turn on your taxi light," make new friends, and see the world while you're at it.

Coaches and masterminds: It's easy for self-reliant solo entrepreneurs to get used to working in a bubble. Investing in a great coach or quality mastermind can counter that tendency by introducing you to new people, ideas, concepts, and strategies, and those connections will more than pay for themselves.

Housekeeping and day care: Listen, you have only so many hours in the day. When you're not working on hustling out your business or growing your side-hustle, the last thing you want to be doing is mowing your lawn, scrubbing your toilets, or trying to keep your child entertained while growing a business. Outsourcing chores and child care will give you the headspace and time to not only make more money in your business but devote more energy outside work to doing the things you love and spending quality time with those you care about most. And if you feel guilty about outsourcing these responsibilities, remember that by doing so, you're supporting the livelihood of others who are trying to make a living by delivering value to your life, too.

Growing your team: If you've been working for yourself for a while, hiring your first employee will feel as scary as the time you quit your day job—but if you're overwhelmed by all the hats you're wearing, growing your team to handle tasks efficiently will be a worthwhile investment. Also, you can dip your toe into growing a team by hiring help as you need it on a project-by-project basis.

BEING A BOSS BOSS

At some point in your boss journey, you'll find yourself in a position in which someone is looking up to you. To her, you're the boss.

It's likely that you'll be her actual boss. As your creative business grows, you will seek out help and begin to expand your team. You'll also find yourself "being the boss" in other capacities, like leading your tribe of followers or becoming an expert or leader in your field. When you find yourself in this position, know that you've made it to the next level.

Most of you are probably here on this journey of independence because you've been miffed by a sucky authority figure in your life—a family member, teacher, or boss at work who didn't measure up to all the high standards we've outlined here thus far, but demanded respect and authority despite blatant shortcomings. Or, perhaps worse, you've had the opportunity to meet people you've admired from afar just to discover that, in real life, they don't live up to your expectations. There can be a disconnect between how people portray themselves and who they actually are in person. But that's not always the case, and it doesn't have to be the case for you. We challenge you to break the mold of bad bosses and disappointing leadership. To embody the ultimate boss persona, you lead by glorious example. You practice good boss skills, not only to push yourself along your own path of fulfillment but also to inspire anyone who may rely on you or look up to you to become the best boss they can be, too.

Here are some qualities that make a really boss boss:
- Punctuality
- Never being above doing even the smallest or grossest of tasks
- Practicing what you preach
- Clearly articulating expectations
- Paying fair wages and checking in regularly with employees
- Expressing gratitude and acknowledging others' efforts

COLLABORATING AND PARTNERING

Finding a collaborator or a partner isn't for everyone; there are many creatives in the world who are meant to build their dreams solo, so don't think that this is a requirement for achieving success. And don't think that finding a partner is the silver bullet for success for your business. No partner is going to dig you out of fear or come to the table to solve all your problems. In other words, don't look for a partner because you're scared or lonely, but rather to help you create something bigger than yourself.

If the idea of collaboration—and opening your vision to someone else's—is appealing to you, bringing on a partner can add new layers and depth to your business. Imagine having someone else as invested in a project or business as you are. Imagine finding someone whose experience matches and complements your own. Imagine splitting the load required to get the job done. What if you had to tend to only half of your garden, while knowing that the other half is getting the same amount of dedicated care? Think about how much bigger you could grow your garden, and how much more care you could give to the smaller portion that you're responsible for.

WHEN WE JOINED FORCES

Kathleen here. Did you hate group assignments in school as much as I did? I craved creative control and seemed to value sleep so much more than my peers, who preferred pulling last-minute all-nighters to finish up the assignment. I love the idea of collaborating, but in practice it can often be frustrating and slow-moving. So, that said, you might be surprised to hear that when Emily pitched me with the idea of starting a podcast together, I enthusiastically said yes. There was no question in my mind that it would be amazing. We had already been working together—she had hired me for branding, and I had hired her for some website development. Furthermore, we had been sharing enough clients to know that our work styles were up to each other's par. We were responsible, on time, and always did the work and pulled our own weight.

Our work ethics and complementary skillsets in creating content, branding, and being tech savvy enough to bootstrap this project certainly set the tone for the work we would do moving forward. We clarified our roles, our goals, and what it was we wanted to create together. And that wasn't a one-time thing. To this day, we consistently check in to see what's working, what's not, and if our vision has evolved. This kind of communication keeps us on the same page and has allowed us to grow beyond our wildest dreams (okay, who am I kidding—we've always had some pretty lofty goals).

It wasn't until we were well on our way to earning six figures in our first year of podcasting together that we knew we needed to get real about what we were creating together. Our passion project had not only become profitable but was building a new kind of potential that required a recalibration of our next moves. We had some good rules, boundaries, and communication in place, but it was clear that we needed a bank account and an operating agreement.

BE A GOOD PERSON

It felt like a really big deal to hire a legit lawyer to handle our operating agreement. Until then, we were working on a handshake and lots of trust. But there came a time for us to get our act together and do the paperwork that would hold up in a court of law, because what would happen if one of us dies tomorrow?! Even more than making our partnership legally binding, going through the operating agreement made us answer a lot of questions we hadn't yet thought of: Will we have a non-compete clause? What *does* happen to *Being Boss* if one of us dies in a plane crash? What happens if one of us decides she wants to quit the business? And, more importantly, what happens if just ONE of us is invited on *Oprah*? Then what?!

The non-compete was tricky because so much of the individual expertise we brought to this new partnership overlapped, and we still had our own individual businesses to consider. A non-compete would require too much nuance and felt like a big can of worms to enact, so instead we asked our lawyer to include a "Be a Good Person" clause in our operating agreement.

Here's exactly what we say in our operating agreement about being a good person and what happens if Oprah calls (and yup, we mention Oprah in our operating agreement):

Each member promises to be a good person. "Good person" means: if something feels funny we have a conversation about it, if we mess up we won't sue each other but we could apologize. We won't say no if Oprah calls, we'll be happy for each other. (But we'll try to get each other on the Oprah show too.)

Our lawyer, who totally gets creative minds and quirks like ours, has since told us that she's been using the "Be a Good Person/Oprah" clause within some of the other operating agreements she's drafted for partnerships ever since!

WHAT KINDS OF SPECIAL CLAUSES WOULD YOU WANT TO PUT IN YOUR PARTNERSHIP AGREEMENT?

You gotta protect what you create

We didn't want this book to get too business-y; we're here to set up the foundations of being boss. But if we're going to encourage you to put yourself out there, we're also going to make sure you're ready to protect what you create. You can figure out a lot of the legal stuff along the way, or you perhaps figured it out long ago. But by working closely with legit counsel, we've learned a lot and wanted to drop some of that knowledge in your hands now in case you want to know what to expect. We've brought in our very own lawyer, Autumn Witt Boyd, to answer a few questions we had in the beginning that might help you too.

BEING BOSS: Hey, Autumn! Let's start with naming your business, services, and products and trademarking. Why is trademarking important? What kinds of things should you consider (legally) when it comes to naming your business?

AUTUMN WITT BOYD: There are two important things to think about when naming your business.

First, pick a good name.

The best choices are fanciful—made-up words that don't mean anything until you build a connection to your product or company with your marketing efforts (like "Kodak" for cameras). The downside here is that you have to do all the work of creating awareness about your product or company, since the name itself doesn't indicate what it's about.

Arbitrary names are also protectable; these are words that have a meaning but are used in a different way (like "Apple" for computers, or "Pandora" for an online music site). Suggestive names ("Being Boss" for a podcast for creative entrepreneurs, or "Groupon" for an online coupon site) give an idea or suggestion of what the business is about without being generic or descriptive and are protected by trademark law.

Avoid names that are descriptive, such as "Jane's Healthy Cookies" for a bakery, "The Complete Personal Branding Guide" for a personal branding course, or "Intuitive Life Coaching" for a coaching business that focuses on using your intuition. In the U.S., these kinds of names are not protected by trademark law until you've used them for long enough that they are well recognized (usually at least five years). So if someone copies the name, you can't do anything legally to stop them until the brand is very well established.

Location-based names, like "Chattanooga Pizza Company," fall into this category as well, as does using your last name, or "surname," so "Smith's Web Design Shop" is not the best choice.

Names that are generic also can't be protected because they just name the thing, such as "The Tire Store" or "Smartphone." In the U.S., these kinds of names are never protected by trademark law, so if someone copies the name, you don't have a legal way to make them stop or change their name.

Second, make sure it's one of a kind. Once you've got a great business or product name, you must check to be sure your name, or a similar name, isn't already being used by another similar business. If a similar business is already using it, they have "priority" rights over the trademark, even if they haven't registered it with the U.S. Patent and Trademark Office. If you start using a trademark someone else owns prior rights to use, you are at risk of getting a nasty cease-and-desist letter or being sued for trademark infringement (even if you later register it with the USPTO!).

I do three searches for my clients:

1. A Google search for the same and similar names

2. A search of the business registry database for the state where the business is located

3. A search of the U.S. Patent and Trademark TESS database

Because trademark law is meant to prevent customer confusion, searching only for the exact name won't ensure that you're in the clear. You should search for alternate spellings and similar words that mean the same thing. (For example, when I searched for my own podcast name, "Legal Road Map," I also checked for "law road map," "lawyer road map," "attorney road map," and variations using "roadmap," "map," "route," and "road," plus plurals and other endings for all of those words, like "maps" or "mapping.")

Checking for domain name or URL availability is not good enough. It's possible to miss a business that operates offline or is using the name in its business or a product but not as its URL.

BB: What's the difference between trademarks and copyright?

AWB: Trademark law protects things that identify the source of a product or service—we usually think of a company or product name, logo, or slogan, but this also includes product packaging and even a sound or color (think Tiffany blue). The goal of trademark law is to allow business owners to build brand recognition and prevent consumers from being confused about the source or quality of a product or service. So, even if someone opens a business with a name that's slightly different from yours, if it's similar enough that it could confuse your customers, then that could be trademark infringement.

Copyright law protects "original works of authorship"—creative works, such as photos, music, books, movies, artwork, software, website content, e-courses, and some jewelry. Copyright law does not protect facts or ideas, only the way facts or ideas are expressed. It can't protect a business system or process, but it can protect the words in a systems manual and documents or worksheets used in the business. The goal of copyright law is to encourage people to create new works, so most copying without permission is considered infringement, unless it falls under "fair use."

BB: When should a creative entrepreneur go ahead and begin the trademark process? It does come at a cost, and if you're trademarking all your ideas willy-nilly, it can add up! How do you begin that process? Should you go ahead and hire someone to help, or can you DIY it?

AWB: After you've chosen a great name and are sure it isn't already in use by someone else, you may want to register it as a nationwide trademark with the U.S. Patent and Trademark Office. This is an investment of time and money in your business—even if you file the application yourself, current USPTO filing fees start at $225 per class, or category, of goods and services (coffee cups are in one class, business consulting is in another class, T-shirts are in another class, and jewelry is in yet another class, so it can add up quickly). The registration process takes a minimum of about nine months if everything goes smoothly, and can take years if any issues come up during the examination or opposition periods.

I ask my clients if it would feel like they were stabbed in the chest if they saw a competitor using the same or similar name, or if they'd lose thousands of dollars if their customers were confused by a similar business or product name. If the answer is yes, my recommendation is that it's time to apply for a federal trademark registration.

I'm a big advocate for entrepreneurs DIY-ing basic legal protections early in their business, but trademark registration is one area where working with a lawyer is the best bet. Because trademark rights are based on use, not registration, a thorough search is a critical first step in the process, and an experienced attorney will be able to help you evaluate your risks if another business is already using a similar name. An attorney will tell you if your business name can't be registered because it's descriptive or generic, before you spend a bunch of money on filing fees for an application that is sure to be denied (the application fees are not refundable!).

And the application process seems straightforward, but is actually full of tricky areas where a simple mistake can cause your application to be denied. I have had several clients come to me after trying to file an application for trademark registration on their own and receiving an office action (a communication from the USPTO attorney that requires a response) with an issue they couldn't fix. This is expensive, and you can lose the ability to register your trademark if another business files an application after yours is denied.

BB: Anything else you want a creative to know about setting themselves up for success when it comes to being legally legit?

AWB: Contracts are the most important legal protection creative entrepreneurs need for their business. They can absolutely write their own contracts when they're getting started, although they may want to consult with a lawyer after they've been in business for a year or more, or are starting to work with bigger or more sophisticated clients or customers. These five terms are key:

1. Detailed list of services or products

2. Itemized and total cost, with clear payment deadlines

3. Refund policy (even if the policy is no refunds, this should be spelled out)

4. How either side can end the relationship, and who gets paid what if it's ended before a project or package is completed

5. Who owns the rights to any intellectual property created as part of the contract

DISCLAIMER: This is information only, and should not be relied upon as legal advice. All information is based on U.S. intellectual property laws.

Autumn Witt Boyd is an experienced lawyer who helps high-achieving and ambitious business owners reach their goals, faster and smarter. Autumn guides creative entrepreneurs with big dreams as they grow from one-person shows to larger deals and collaborations. She has special expertise in copyright and trademark issues. Autumn also hosts the Legal Road Map *podcast, which teaches business owners how to protect their rights and stay out of legal hot water. She lives in Chattanooga, Tennessee, with her husband, Dave, twin boys, Sam and Tyson, and daughter, Vivian.*

HARD CONVERSATIONS AND GOOD COMMUNICATION

While we don't think you need a fancy business plan to start a business, if you plan on partnering with someone you need to begin with what resembles an operating agreement ASAP. Good communication will eliminate the need for intense conversations and nip any resentment in the bud. Regularly chatting about what you do (and don't) want with your values, intentions, and boundaries in mind will keep everyone on the same page and working toward the same goal.

Before you ever pursue a partnership or collaboration, you need to be able to have a conversation about the following questions:
- What are your roles and expectations?
- How will you handle disagreements?
- What can you imagine would cause a disagreement?
- What are your shared goals?
- How do your individual values support your shared goals?
- How will you split money? How will you handle expenses?
- What happens if something feels like a conflict of interest?
- Do you have a non-compete agreement in place?
- Who owns the intellectual property? Who has rights in the project?
- What happens to the business if one of you quits or dies?
- What's your communication style?
- How do you handle stress?

If discussing any of these topics feels too awkward to broach or results in a heated conversation, you might want to rethink the partnership. It doesn't mean you don't like each other or can't be friends, but it may mean you're not a good fit as business partners. And especially once money is involved, it is a good idea to get an agreement on paper and signed by all parties involved in a project—no matter how small the collaboration may be. Remember, having hard conversations is a practice, and the more you communicate with the people in your life, the easier those chats will become.

FINDING YOUR BUSINESS BESTIE

You don't necessarily need a business partner to battle loneliness or help you fix your business—you may just need a business bestie! Think about someone you enjoy talking shop with. He or she has a work ethic and drive that matches your own. You will share advice and support each other along the way. It's important to note that your business bestie is NOT a mentor or coach—while you and your business bestie may mentor or coach each other, it's ultimately an equal exchange. Think about who you already know who fits the profile and schedule regular Skype or coffee dates with that person.

Your business bestie is someone you can confide in on a regular basis about stuff like this:

MONEY GOALS: It's often seen as taboo to talk numbers, but you'll want to get specific with your business bestie about how much money you make and how much you'd like to be making.

INTENTIONS AND INSIGHTS: Create a monthly intention or focus and share it with your business bestie. Brainstorm how you can carry this intention into your work and hold each other accountable for living your values.

STRATEGIES: What's working in your business? You and your business bestie can exchange tactics for marketing your latest launches and growing your following, or trade secrets on how to close deals with potential clients.

STRUGGLES AND VICTORIES: Have a tricky issue that has you blocked? Bring it to your business bestie! And on the flip side, be sure to celebrate your big and little wins with your business bestie.

It is possible for you to make money doing things that you love, but you gotta do the work.

- YOU DON'T NEED A COMPLICATED BUSINESS PLAN, BUT YOU NEED TO KNOW HOW YOU'RE GOING TO MAKE MONEY.

- WHAT DO YOU WANT TO BE KNOWN FOR?

- WHAT TOOLS ARE IN YOUR TOOLBELT?

- DO YOU HAVE A VISION FOR HAVING A BUSINESS PARTNER? IF SO, HOW WILL YOU BOTH GET ON THE SAME PAGE WHEN IT COMES TO GROWING A PROFITABLE BUSINESS?

- WHOM DO YOU CONFIDE IN WHEN IT COMES TO TALKING SHOP? DO YOU HAVE A BUSINESS BESTIE?

CHAPTER 6:

Live your life

Do the work so you can live your life— on your terms.

We're not trying to tell you how to live your life, but we can definitively say that being a workaholic isn't cool—no matter how passionate you are about your job. The danger of being a creative entrepreneur is that because we love what we do so much, we tend to prioritize work above everything else. Plus, when your work is an expression of who you are, it's easy to tie your self-worth directly to your bottom line. A lot rides on the work that we do, from paying the bills to creative fulfillment, and we're not just trying to make a paycheck doing what we love—we're trying to make a life worth living.

As creative entrepreneurs, we know that in our work we need to be nimble, to make decisions based on our values, and to be able to reinvent ourselves on the fly in order to keep up with the demands of an evolving economy and personal vision. And as creatives, it's important we apply that same kind of desire and tenacity to our lives outside of work.

In this chapter we're going to talk about creating a life you love and remembering what you're really working for.

WHO DO YOU WANT TO BE?

Your entire body regenerates every seven years. Your skeleton is replaced every decade; your skin replaces itself every two to three weeks; and some of our cells, like those in our stomach lining and intestines, replace themselves on the daily. There's something comforting in the idea that we physically get to be a new person every day, week, and decade—and I love the idea that as bosses we can choose who we want to be today, tomorrow, and the day after that.

Take a moment to reflect on where you've been, what you've learned along the way, and how far you've come. Divide your life into seven-year increments and write down what you learned, what milestones you hit, what struggles you faced, and what accomplishments you achieved in each of those seven years. It's going to feel like a lot—but that's the point. So often it seems we're getting nowhere in our day-to-day lives, but when you are able to really see how much you accomplish, learn, and do in the span of seven years, it will give you a fresh perspective on what you're achieving, learning, and doing right now.

Who do you want to be in the next seven years? What do you want to learn? What do you want to achieve? How do you want to behave in the face of challenges?

Who you want to be in the next seven years begins today. So every morning when you wake up, ask yourself, "What will make me feel most like *me*?" Whether it's the outfit you wear, the conversations you have, the places you go, or the kind of work you create . . . it's up to you to be who you are and consciously choose who you will become.

LIFE HUSTLE

Life hustle is the most fun. It is all the things you *work* for so that you can *do,* like taking vacations or building your dream house. But really living your life also includes the little things, like waking up on Saturday morning to do your grocery shopping or taking your kid to piano practice.

You have to put some effort into life in order to harvest and enjoy the fruits of your work. And this harvest and enjoyment are anything but passive. Nothing rewarding ever comes easily. Life requires just as much focus and dedication and as many boundaries and routines as work hustle, but it's not done for the currency of money. It's done for the currency of sheer fulfillment.

Here are some examples of life hustles that will make you feel like a boss outside of work:
- Vacationing with family or friends
- Having children
- Baking bread from scratch
- Holding dinner parties

- Gardening
- Going on an adventure
- Learning how to dance
- Volunteering for a cause you support
- Decluttering your home
- Going on a spirit quest

DO WHAT YOU WANT

Our biggest fear is living a life of full of regret, stagnation, and fear. We see far too many creatives living based on societal "shoulds" and niceties. But we want you to do what you want. Whether that's launching a creative career on your own or jumping out of an airplane, life is yours to grab by the horns. But just like owning what you want and making it happen in business, you have to know what you want in life. And you gotta get specific.

TRY THIS: MAKE A "BUCKET LIST" of at least 100 things you want to do, places you want to go, and things you want to try before you die. (A hundred might feel like a lot of things to do—it's okay if you get only twenty on your first go at it—just keep building on as you go.)

INDIE GOES WEST

Many bosses we know dream of selling off their possessions, packing up their car, and hitting the road on an epic journey. And in 2015, that's exactly what I did.

Emily here. We called this great American road trip that lasted forty days #indiegoeswest to pay homage to the business I had built—Indie Shopography—that helped me turn this life goal into a reality. And also because being independent and doing what I see as fit for myself is my way of life, and it was taking me west.

My partner and I were already planning an out-of-state move for the summer of 2015 when, in the spring before we began packing up, we got the wild idea to spend the time between packing our old house and buying our new house on a cross-country road trip with our daughter and our dog. A long-term road trip like this had been on our wish list for years; our daughter was finally old enough to endure such an adventure, and our change in living situation made it a prime time to dip out for a few weeks of wandering around America.

For my business, it was also an opportunity for me to test out how well I had built it. I had been nurturing a team that could manage most things while I was away, and we made plans to touch base every few days. For the *Being Boss* podcast, we prerecorded over a month of content, setting me up to leave with my work already done. The trip was the realization of my creative entrepreneur dream: traveling with my family, working from the road, and still building my business along the way.

In case you need ideas for what to put on your bucket list, here are just a few of ours:

EMILY'S BUCKET LIST

- BACKPACK THROUGH EUROPE
- WRITE A COCKTAIL BOOK
- HAVE A TINY HOUSE (OR GLASS MANSION) IN THE WOODS
- ADOPT A REDWOOD GROVE
- LEARN HOW TO LIGHT CANDLES WITH THE SNAP OF A FINGER!

KATHLEEN'S BUCKET LIST

- SEE THIS BOOK YOU'RE READING ON THE SHELF AT AN AIRPORT

- LIVE ON THE EAST COAST OF AUSTRALIA FOR THREE MONTHS

- ATTEND MAKEUP SCHOOL IN NYC OR PARIS

- LEARN THE CHOREOGRAPHY TO A HIT BEYONCÉ SONG

- HAVE A FAMILY PORTRAIT TAKEN OF OUR AURAS

It all fell into place with remarkable ease. But the trip itself pushed me in ways that I never imagined.

This adventure tested parts of my primal programming I've never encountered before, especially providing basic needs for my family (i.e., where we'd eat our next meal or where we'd hang our hat for the night). This adventure was the epitome of a life hustle. In forty days we drove 10,000 miles, visited twenty-two states, toured dozens of our national treasures, hiked, cooked over a fire, and slept on the ground. We showered once a week, carried only as much food as would fit in a small cooler, and rarely knew where we would sleep until about an hour before we arrived at our campsite for the night. Long-term camping is hard enough, but setting up and taking down camp every day is its own kind of grueling work. Going extended periods of time without all the things that make life easier is something I had never experienced before. Not to mention I spent forty days hovering over toilets that were little more than holes in the ground with little shacks built on top of them. I became a master of the chair pose, and I can go from gear-explosion to ready-to-hit-the-road in less than an hour.

We adjusted our mindset, set up boundaries, and adopted new habits and routines throughout the entire trip. It was the realization of a goal we'd held for years, and reaching the end of it intact was a goal we maintained throughout the entire trip. We worked hard for both of those goals, and it changed our ability to hustle forever, in life and in work. I knew it would change how I worked with people and how I held myself accountable to get shit done. When #indiegoeswest was complete, we were all different people. That life hustle made me more boss than any work hustle ever could, and rewarded me in ways that my business never will.

HOW TO SET UP YOUR BUSINESS TO TAKE TIME OFF FOR YOUR LIFE HUSTLE

Whether you're planning an epic vacation, a honeymoon, or even maternity leave, you can put processes in place to keep your business running smoothly in your absence:

Create and schedule content in advance: If you are regularly blogging, podcasting, or sending out emails to your newsletter list, be sure to write or record material in advance and schedule it to post while you're gone.

Set up auto-responders to your email: Let people who are trying to reach you know where you're going (you can make it fun and personable!) and when you plan to be back.

Wrap up projects, orders, and to-dos: You might be busting ass to get it all done before you head out, but you'll leave with the peace of mind that you'll be coming home to a clean slate.

Budget accordingly: If you're taking a week, a month, or even a good portion of your year off, be sure to plan for that pause in income.

Let your clients or customers know you'll be on hiatus: If you're a one-person shop, you'll especially want to let recurring customers or retainer clients know that you'll be unavailable.

Staff up: One of the best things about having employees is that someone is there to hold down the fort while you're out.

BEING BOSS WITH KIDS

Living a life you love can include some grand adventures—from hiking the Himalayas to taking an epic road trip, but we don't want to paint a picture of a life hustle that is just about the big adventures that make a great story. Sometimes the most challenging and rewarding life moments happen in the daily grind—especially with the endurance it takes to be a parent.

There's a lot of guilt that naturally shows up when you're trying to balance being present as a parent with focusing on your career—but growing a business and growing a family don't have to be mutually exclusive. In our experience, being parents has helped us, in many ways, become better bosses. On the flip side, the lessons we've learned in business, from setting boundaries to establishing productive habits and routines for managing time, have directly contributed to how we're able to balance the responsibilities that come with being parents. There are a lot of parallels between raising a kiddo and building a business:

You have to be adaptable: One of the fastest lessons you'll learn in business and parenthood alike is that not everything always goes as planned. You might daydream about working from home with a baby playing with wooden toys in a crisp white onesie. Any parent knows firsthand that the onesie will not stay crisp and white. There are lots of parents who can finesse the work-from-home situation (kudos to you), but you might find that it's really hard to be a parent and be a boss *at the same time*. You have to adapt your dreamy visions and be able to pivot when things change, in both work and life, according to your actual circumstances.

You may feel nothing will ever be enough: When business is personal, you'll find yourself feeling that you could always be doing more and better. The same is true with kids. But you can't be too precious or protective with either one. Your business, like your child, in many ways has a life of its own. You can't control every little aspect, and where would the fun be in that anyway?

Multitasking is a joke: In work you'll quickly learn that without focus, balls will be dropped, deadlines will be missed, and important emails will fall through the cracks. The same is true at home—if you're trying to cook dinner while catching up on said emails and running a bath at the same time, something is going to get burnt (or flooded).

It's not always fun: The part about being a parent and working for yourself that everyone is always too ashamed to admit is that it's not always fun.

We glamorize both parenting and entrepreneurship with curated Instagram feeds and Pinterest-perfect snapshots, but in reality, building a business and growing a family is complex and far more messy than we let on.

All that said, what those curated Instagram snaps fail to capture are the nuances and depth of experience that our life and work hustle gives us. It's not always fun, nor should it be! The tenacity, grit, and endurance that come with hustling out some life—from the daily grind to the daring adventures—are what make us so damn boss.

And finally, if you need a reminder that you're doing a great job (most parents and entrepreneurs do), consider this your pep talk.

WHERE'S YOUR KID WHILE YOU WORK?

Child care is one of the biggest issues that parents have to face, whether they work for someone else or for themselves. And being an entrepreneur doesn't actually make this decision any easier. In fact, it probably makes it harder, because you *do* have the option of keeping your kid with you while you work, whereas that's much less likely if you have a day job.

Emily here. In my years of working for myself as a mom, I've tried out every single child care option for my daughter, except boarding school. (We're still waiting on her Hogwarts letter, so even that's not ruled out yet.) Early in her life, grandparents played a large role in keeping her safe and fed when I needed to get work done. At two different times I've had a nanny of sorts come into my home multiple times a week to entertain her while I tackled my task list in another room. When she was ready for pre-K, she attended part-time. For kindergarten, she went to school like all the other kids. Now, we homeschool; David handles our daughter's education and is the primary caregiver while I'm writing, recording, and coaching.

Every phase of our care for our daughter has been a product of our lifestyle and—honestly—what we could afford. Depending on where we lived, what resources were available, our own work demands, and her age and needs, our requirements for taking care of our kid have shifted. When needs changed, so did our arrangements. We make the best decision we can with the options that we have, and it's your job to do the same. Feeling guilty about any decision, no matter what it may be, is a waste of energy as long as your decisions are fully considered with all the boss foundations in place: what's most important to you, what rules will support that, and how can you adjust your daily routine to make sure it all works?

You must tackle parenthood the same way you tackle living and working like a boss. Don't live by anyone else's standards; do what is right for you and your family. Know what you want to get out of your family life, and make the decisions and take the actions that will help you reach your goals. Set expectations, but stay open to allow things to bloom in ways that you couldn't even imagine. Enjoy what you have, and do the work.

TREAT YO'SELF!

Self-care is getting a lot of buzz these days. It should be obvious that we need to take care of the number one asset in our work and life (ourselves!). However, there are still far too many people who wear their eighty-hour work weeks and sleep deprivation like a badge of honor. Not cool. So we don't mind if self-care is a trend and we all bring a little more attention to treating our bodies, minds, relationships, and spirits like the bosses we are. Plus, a regular self-care practice will help you cope with the stress and challenges that inevitably come with running a business while having a life.

Self-care can be integrated into your morning and nightly routine, but it's also about truly treating yourself to some indulgences you deserve. Be sure to schedule weekly or monthly self-care appointments, and treat them like any other important meeting! And don't let the cost of self-care be an excuse not to treat yourself. We love splurging when we can, but there are lots of inexpensive and totally free ways to indulge yourself, too:

- Hug someone you love—it will boost those feel-good hormones.
- Book a vacation and leave your laptop at home.
- Take yourself on a date to the museum.
- Get a new plant to put in your garden.
- Upgrade to first class on that flight.
- Get a massage.
- Invest in a monthly subscription box of goodies (like clothes, food, or beauty products).
- Get it on with yourself (or someone you love).
- Read a magazine while drinking your favorite beverage.
- Buy yourself fresh flowers.
- Get a mani-pedi.
- Enjoy a face mask.
- Put your bare feet in some grass and maybe hug a tree.

How would you treat yourself?

MAKING FRIENDS AS A GROWN-UP

It's been said that we are the sum of the five people we hang out with most. Whether or not that's true, it's really important that you surround yourself with people who are going to challenge you to be and support you in being your best self.

Write down the five people you hang out with the most:

1. _____

2. _____

3. _____

4. _____

5. _____

What do they value? What's their disposition? What are they really talented at? Where do they struggle? Now it's time to get really honest with yourself. Are you hanging out with the kind of people who support and inspire you? Or are your friends lowering your vibes? What do you bring to the relationships you have? Are you being the kind of friend you'd like to be?

That's a lot of questions. You might be saying, "Okay. I need to fill my life with more high-vibing creatives!" and after that, you might be asking, "But where do I find them!?" Good question. It's not always easy to make friends as a grown-ass adult, but we've got a few ideas for you:

• **Join a club!** There are a lot of professional associations in every industry where you can meet like-minded creatives.

• **Take a class.** Local workshops, remote retreats, and even small conferences where you're learning something new or honing your craft with other people offer great opportunities to find your tribe.

• **Invite someone you admire to coffee.** Okay, this one might feel a little bold, but you might already have an acquaintance who would make for a great friend. Muster up your courage and invite them on a coffee or dinner date.

• **Get out of your house.** You're never going to meet new people if you're holed up in your home office. You might have to leave your comfort zone to make new friends, whether that means sitting on your front porch and engaging with your neighbors or joining a co-working space.

• **Make friends online.** Some of our closest relationships started by commenting on someone's blog or Instagram post—the trick here is you can't just be a lurker. You have to engage in conversations with people you like.

New relationships can begin from the smallest spark and grow into lifelong friendships. From meeting new people to sustaining long-term

Celebrate with jewelry

We're admittedly not great about congratulating ourselves and celebrating #bossmoments and big wins. As soon as we hit our goal, we raise the bar, and we're often too busy mapping out our plan of attack to acknowledge how far we've come. Plus, we do a pretty good job of regularly treating ourselves to little indulgences *just because* . . . so a "cheers" with a glass of bubbly doesn't always seem to do our big wins the justice they deserve. We were sharing our struggle to properly celebrate with a creative peer when she told us how she acknowledges her milestone accomplishments: she buys herself a meaningful piece of jewelry. That way she gets a beautiful accessory as well as a constant reminder of good work done.

relationships, making and keeping friends is a habit you have to practice and nurture. Set up a regular reminder to text, call, or email the people who are important to you. Invite people you want to spend more time with to a monthly meetup or weekly dinner party. Stay connected with people who are meaningful to you, and they will bring more meaning and fulfillment to your life.

Connection is everything. Nurturing relationships is how you keep those connections alive and well. When you push your relationships aside for the sake of your to-do list, then you're sacrificing the part of your life that will leave you feeling the most rich.

Healthy relationships are:
• Mutually beneficial
• Supportive and inspiring
• Honest
• Full of laughter

BE A STUDENT OF LIFE

When we listen to podcasts, read books, and scan profiles in business magazines featuring big-name bosses, it's easy to recognize what they have in common: a killer work ethic, a solid morning routine, and an insatiable appetite for growth. We're not talking obsessing-over-the-bottom-line kind of growth—we're talking about being a student of life. The entrepreneurs we admire not only live by a code of ethics and a tight sense of integrity, but are dedicated to learning more, honing their craft, and raising the bar for themselves every single day. Even the smartest experts will humbly admit to not knowing it all, but won't stop trying to soak up as much knowledge as they can until the day they die. And they're not just taking courses and continuing their education in a formal manner. They're learning lessons from the books they always have on their bedside table, the stories they hear from friends and peers, and the life they're living.

Students of life are committed to living lives full of experience, expansion, and exploration. To grow, you have to be open to change and willing to try new things and think new ideas. Being a student of life comes back to setting an intention and keeping your eyes peeled for lessons along the way. And it's not just about learning new things to apply to your business (though as a student of life you most certainly will learn new tools, tactics, and concepts you can apply to your creative career). Being a student of life is about exploring the things you're curious about. And that's what makes people well-rounded, memorable, and interesting—beyond the work they do.

TRY THIS: THE NEXT TIME YOU'RE NETWORKING OR MEETING NEW PEOPLE, instead of asking them what they do, try asking them what they're curious about, what they're reading, or what they've learned recently.

A FINAL SEND-OFF . . .

Trust that if you do the work and actually begin implementing the mindset, habits, routines, boundaries, tools, and actionable tactics we've written about in this book, you can reap the rewards of being boss. But you gotta do the work!

We want to send you on your way knowing this: Being boss is a lifelong commitment and an exciting ride. Cultivating confidence takes practice, but slowly you'll collect evidence that you can do this, which will only continue to propel you forward. Being who you are 100 percent of the time, owning your shit, making money in a way that reflects your values, being creatively fulfilled, and living a good life along the way will only happen when you get intentional about what you want and making it happen.

The work of being boss is never done—you're always on your entrepreneurial path, and so are we. Our stories began at an advertising agency and a tanning salon, and there were lots of chapters in the middle that led us to create a chart-topping podcast and write an actual book (thanks for reading!). But we're not done yet! This is just one more chapter along the way. What's next? We don't know. We hope to become best-selling authors (if you liked this book, give us a good review and buy one for your friends!). We're hoping Oprah calls to invite us over for lunch. We can't help but daydream about what it would be like to have a TV show. We have big dreams, but being boss is more than just thinking about big ass goals and best-case scenarios. We're hustling every day to do the work, and resting (or taking an amazing vacation) when we need it. We've made plenty of space on our chalkboard, but we're also focusing on enjoying the process and embracing the uncertainty that comes with being your own boss. We're in it with you and using the same tips and tactics we shared with you here in this book to get there.

Do the work.
Be boss.

ACKNOWLEDGMENTS AND THANK-YOUS

Special thanks to our agent Laura Lee Mattingly—you got us and our vision from the beginning. To our editor Jennifer Kasius and the entire Running Press team who helped us bring our first book into the world. Huge thanks to all our friends and peers who contributed to this book. And to the *Being Boss* team: Caitlin, Sharon, Corey, Liz, Autumn, and Brigitte—we couldn't have done it without you. Big thanks to Sarah Becker Lillard for always making us look so good—and to our models Sara and AJ! To our mentors, coaches, and wolf pack who have been with us every step of the way—you know who you are. To our family who supported us while we busted out our deadlines—David, Lily, Jeremy, Fox, and Tara—a million thanks wouldn't be enough. And of course to our *Being Boss* podcast listeners and partners—thank you!

Index

Pryor, Jay, 125, 127
publishing, 147–148

quitting, 55

reading list, 75
reality, 114, 117, 124, 166
recognition, 45
rejections, 63
relationships, 30, 70–71, 85 (fig.), 188, 190
resilience, 49
respect, 100
responsibility, 53, 60, 70, 164
rest, 27, 45, 82, 93, 96, 133, 187
   sleep, 115–116, 119
rituals, 120, 134–138
road trip, 181, 184
Robbins, Tony, 63, 131
routines, 30, 107, 116, 132
   morning, 109–110, 112–113
   rituals, 134–138

schedule, 28, 101
science experiment, decision-making as, 65–66, 67 (fig.)
security, 9, 43
self, 54, 60, 75, 157
   employee handbook for, 92, 94
   investment in, 163, 165–166
   success and, 98–99
self-care, 93, 111, 187
   health care compared to, 118–119
self-criticism, 52–53
self-definition, 80

self-deprecation, 52, 116
self-doubt, 26, 55, 58
self-esteem, 57
self-love, 61
self-talk, negative, 52–53
Sethi, Ramit, 31
sharing, 49
Shih, Jenny, 98–99
Shinn, Florence Scovel, 116
sleep, 115–116, 119
social media, 83, 95, 108
space, 125–127, 165
   orbit exercise, 70–71, 71 (fig.)
   "white," 84, 85 (fig.), 86
   See also goal-setting
Spencer, Ezzie, 136–137
spoken boundaries, 100
spoken content, 151
spoken intentions, 135
strategies, 25, 174
Street, Tara, 156–157
success, 98–99
   goal-setting for, 124–129, 128 (fig.)
   overnight, 18–19
sugar, 115

tanning salon, 14–15
Tate, Tisha, 74
taxi light, 62
tea ritual, 120
teamwork, 49, 166
technology, 163, 165
telephone, 97
thoughts, 68, 72, 116
time, 51, 135–137